RUNNING
the SEVEN
CONTINENTS

Tales of Travel and the Marathon

To George
Here's to the journey

Clint Morrison

Clint Morrison
Whidbey Island Marathon
April 2007

PORTLAND • OREGON
INKWATERPRESS.COM

Front cover, bottom symbols represent the number "seven" in seven different mathematical systems, from left to right: Mayan (North America), Sino-Japanese (Asia), Nagari (India), International "Arabic" (Antarctica), Coptic (Africa), Roman (Europe), and seven knots on a rope, the Inca quipu (South America).

The encounters with actual persons in these adventures are described as the author recalls them. Many of the names, but not all of them, have been changed. The descriptions of these encounters are not intended to exalt, blame, offend, or impress the persons concerned. We were wayfarers in the same place and time and the author begs your indulgence.

Running the Seven Continents: Tales of Travel and the Marathon
Copyright © 2006 by Clint Morrison

Photos and maps © 2006 Clint Morrison
Front cover cover: Top: author running, Yukon River and Lake Kawaguchi photographer unknown, Bottom: Neko Harbor, Antarctica, photo by Clint Morrison. Back cover, top: Hout Bay, South Africa, photo by Clint Morrison, bottom: Death Valley photographer unknown.

Cover and interior design by Masha Shubin
Edited by Linda Weinerman

www.inkwaterpress.com

ISBN-10 1-59299-237-4
ISBN-13 978-1-59299-237-9

Publisher: Inkwater Press

Printed in the U.S.A.

To my parents, for the start,
to my wife, for the journey,
and to my children, for the roads that lie ahead

Table of Contents

Prologue

Set out on a journey and let it claim you.

This is not a decision to clean the house, rake leaves, or mow the lawn. Not a decision to go to the park, or the pool, or the gym.

Be in another place, where you would not be. See something that matters. Something that cannot be seen from home. Set the starting line wherever you choose, but set it far from home. Hail other travelers or travel alone, but only you will take your journey. Light footfalls on pine needles, cement slabs, gravel or mud that only you can cause. Turns in the road that only you will see with shadow and clearing set by your direction and at your time of day. If a tree falls in the forest, you will hear it.

Run.
Back to the Eden before there was success and failure, wealth and penury, love and rejection.
Back to the spring of life, when feet raced over sidewalks or playgrounds and off to the chase or back to the teacher or out to play or home to dinner and there was always enough life in the cup for another race, another game, another sprint.

Run forward to the bend in the road, see where the course goes from there.

Forward to a time of wisdom, of having seen where it all leads, having run the course and felt the curvature of the earth beneath our feet.

Forward to a time of hope that knowledge can bring understanding. To the day when all people are again brothers and sisters and call off conflict, and greet each other acknowledging past struggles but also the humanity that all share in common.

One leans before the first step. A tilt in posture, a wish to be elsewhere, and the foot is poised to strike. A shift in that direction, the step is taken and the journey begins.

Run on the bright grass damp with the morning, the spring of the new earth under your stride. The sun young for this day glistens on the turf, frames your running shadow with a halo of brightness. Each footfall comes across rolling green grass, hill and gully, springing up to the crown and speeding down the far side, over patches of dirt and rock, past side roads, a stand of trees, a fence, a sign of water, a track of birds.

As your legs stretch and warm to the task, wind fills your ears like a chorus. The sky approves, the warmth of the sun is welcome. The pace is yours, your air fills lungs, pumps the heart red and rich to toes and arms and eyes and mind. The eye records, the mind sees, the feet trace the surface. The earth has no end, forever. Sights are to follow, to explore to the source and beyond, to more hills and to still farther views from the heights.

The sun stands still in the heavens.

Crest each hill, spot each new goal in the distance. Reach it, find a new one. Go. Until at last you see that there must be a turning point. Choose a landmark whence to loop back with a last look at the horizon. Turn. But look up, for the way back has views to offer, now less familiar in a slowly changing light. The dew may long since have vanished but the footprints of the outward morning are still here and there. Slopes once sprinted take a little longer to ascend, and on the downhill side there are slight discomforts in a knee, an ankle. The sun has moved after all, and now falls again over the shoulder. The stride is shorter. Slant light shadows the way ahead even as the scene leaps into the bright focus of late afternoon.

Doubt, at first lightly then in earnest, the legs' ability to go the last miles. The rise and fall of the land is no longer easy, the breath short, and the heart no longer as able as in the morning, yet the senses are sharper. Coax another curve, another rise, out of tired muscles and spent vigor. Tell the mind that warmth and rest and waters await but not yet. Scold, promise, invent, slow, but keep going ahead. Every stride passes some object of wonder, a leaf, rock, stand of roadside grass etched in the glow of light from the west.

Just as daylight begins to fade in earnest, as the true night extends from the top of the last hill, raise the frame to its true height and feel the legs pick up a bit of the kick of the morning. Grasp the ground with a purpose. Now there is half a mile to go, now three hundred yards. Now.

End the journey with gratitude, warmth, rest, water. Walk for a moment. More sound and sight is recorded behind your eyelids than in front of them. Look clearly at the sights that only you have seen at this hour and the distance that only you have covered, today. Whatever lies behind you is now further behind. And in a few moments and for the rest of life, become where you went and what you have seen.

Foreword

The concept of the Seven Continent Marathon Adventure

Once the marathon was considered the ultimate test of endurance. The distance itself has not changed, but our perception of it has been altered. The marathon runner in 1900 was a rare species. Today more runners have completed 100-mile and longer races than had run marathons a hundred years ago. Travel across geographic, cultural, and political barriers is also far easier today than a century ago.

The first steps, always the hardest, occurred somewhat naturally for me. While I was living on other continents in 1983 and 1984, my introduction to marathon running was fueled by inner efforts to deal first with life in a Japanese accounting office and later with three months of extended business travel and living alone out of a suitcase in Australia.

Ten years passed before I attempted marathons again. I ran at Chicago in 1994. By then the global career I had aimed at was a thing of the past and, feeling isolated through my wife's sabbatical year, I devised a return to running as a clever way to deal with my new concerns. It brought a new level of physical challenge, and also burnished and prolonged the modest degree of athletic ability I do possess. It got me under the qualifying time for the Boston Marathon for the only time in my life, and I duly made sure that I ran that year, in 1996. We made it a family event and my wife even flew back for the occasion, all the way from Seoul.

I had now run on three continents. Training and traveling to distant marathons was feeling like a clever way to supply the global span and sense of purpose that I felt had been sacrificed in my choice of family rather than career. I read that runners had gone to the Antarctic to run a marathon and would do so again in early 1997, and I saw the opportunity to temporarily balance my sense of equality in my marriage, and to eventually complete the Seven Continents. There was even a whiff of romance associated with such a quest. It would not bring riches, but then it wasn't terribly expensive either, and it is important to me that most of my journeys were financed chiefly by game-fees from seasonal soccer officiating and by birthday and holiday gifts from family, rather than out of the general household budget. This made it truly my own hobby undertaking, and demonstrates that the Seven Continents can be done without tremendous expenses or going into debt.

My wife could not go along to Antarctica but did meet me in Buenos Aires on my return, and we spent a wonderful week together in the late Argentine summer, celebrating 25 years together.

There were other marathon and longer runs in North America, at Portland, Death Valley, Whitehorse, and in the trails of the Oregon Cascades. Once Antarctica was behind me, it remained to identify, plan, and execute three more marathon trips even as the world began to accelerate into new and more frightening times.

Africa came in 1999 as President Nelson Mandela prepared to leave office. In 2001, before the fires of September 11 were out, I changed my plans to run in New York and chose Athens instead for its historic and symbolic significance. Then in 2002, feeling my long-distance running days approaching an end, I discovered southern Brazil and ran in the island city of Florianopolis.

Acknowledgments

Thanks and appreciation are due first of all to my wife Nancy, not only for enduring the sweaty running clothes, countless pairs of shoes and irregular absences suffered by all who live with runners, but also for famously being the one who first suggested that running on all the continents might be a goal I could shoot for. And to my parents for encouraging and supporting me at important times.

Thanks to the late George Sheehan for suggesting that a good pair of orthotics could keep me running, to Kathy Sherwood for making and servicing them, and to Dr. Stephen Roy for creative and insightful medical diagnoses. And to the Asics shoe company for maintaining consistency and quality in their products for so many years.

Thanks too, to my children Elise, Ted, and Laura, well used to knowing that "Dad's out running," and by now embarked on lives of adventure each in their own way. To the Oregon State University "Nooners," an informal source of running challenges, philosophy, historical perspective and humor for well over a decade, for making it easy to turn fifty and now address the turning of sixty and beyond. In no particular order, Jeff, Jim, Roland, Greg, Phil, Mike, Clem, Bill, John, Dave, Boone, Peter,

Ken, Jack, Bob, Cliff, Deb, Meghan, Gaby, Susan, Kim, Linda, and many others, thanks.

Thanks also for cooperation and information to:
Community Relations Office, University of Texas El Paso

North America

The Yukon River Trail, in the second half of the marathon
(photographer unknown).

Yukon River Trail Marathon
August 2001

YUKON:
The route of the 1999 Yukon River Trail Marathon.
The course goes south up the Yukon River, crosses the
suspension bridge at Miles Canyon, then follows trails
past rivers, woods, and lakes and eventually back to
the center of Whitehorse.

CHAPTER 1

Eat Here or We'll Both Starve

Yukon River Trail Marathon, August 2001

> *...it isn't the gold that I'm wanting*
> *So much as just finding the gold."*
>
> Robert W. Service, *The Spell of the Yukon*

I

Early Tuesday morning: Portland bus. Light gray overcast, daylight by five forty-five. Clean streets, summer morning greenery heavy on the trees. Wet port air by the river. A woman speaking only Spanish wants to call a number that is not answering at an address in NE Portland. No more time to help, I have to board the bus. Downtown brick streets, renovated store fronts, huge glass panes with black trim. The old side of an apartment building shows a faded ad for Columbia Window Shades.

Two black men at the door talk in deep voices, projecting. "I got lucky, I went to Japan."

"Oh, so they put you in support, right?"

A sparrow flits around in the closed arcade of the terminal. An infant strains out from its mother's arms, seeing the bird hopping on the floor, and the infant coos. The bird picks at a sandwich near some spilled orange juice. An older sister, maybe two, says yuck and mother says "Birds like that." Someone observes that the bird will be inside the terminal for a long time.

I'm off and winging, though, bag tagged to Bellingham, myself poised on the branch and about to fly, solo in the clear liquid that we all breathe but seldom do I get to test to see if it will bear my weight. Jack London, White Fang, Dan McGrew, Sam McGee, here I come. Lights off on the bus, gun the motor, and edge into traffic at the corner of 6th and Glisan, Harvey's Comedy Lounge. Already my daughter, who dropped me off, is not here. The car is gone. We all fly routes of our own choosing.

A green freighter, marked MISR Shipping Line, is at a grain terminal on the east side of the river. She is the *Esna*, from Egypt.

It's an eight-minute burst of freedom, no more. The bus pulls off immediately at Vancouver, across the river. "We'll be here five minutes. If you step off and smoke, stay twenty feet clear of the bus." So that's why the five-minute stopovers are identified on the itinerary. "Sounds like a plaaaaan to me!" sings a female voice from the back. Tobacco smoke wafts into the open front door. Across the street are Main Street Loan and Pawn Shop, Mike's Loans, and the Lucky Loan Pawn Shop. In a few minutes we are rolling again.

I-5 is six lanes wide, flanked by small groups of trees and farms. Two young men, a balding bespectacled blond and an Army private type, are regaling two young women with loud stories and suggestive jokes, to giggles of appreciation and attempts at repartee. I'm too far away to hear the content of the talk, too near to ignore it. They are playing a scene, each posing and acting and checking the response before going on to the next line. The private has the main role and apparently the best stories. The young kids on the bus are all asleep, tucked sideways across double seats.

I have put one foot out the door on other occasions before this, to run away, to run towards, to run. A few miles in the park or a couple of hours on forest trails suffice to put me back in a contented state. This time the need to escape is deeper. It has been mostly my own fault. I took a summer math class, setting out to learn differential equations, the abstract truths that connect impetus with motion and distance or link food supply with population changes. But I fell behind in the class. Then I was careless, and had my book, notes, and backpack stolen just before the midterm. I got angry at life and others, well beyond the threshold of restlessness. This time both feet went out the door. Differential equations will have to wait. Now I will ask the open road for education, and trust that in the light of the day and a few words with others along the way there will be enough to make the journey worthwhile. The tools of my trade are my shoes. The pretext is to go to a land once considered the limit of habitation, to run a distance once considered the limit of human endeavor. But the journey there and back will be a training run in the best sense.

The sky gets darker, pillows of deep gray. The road is wet. At Kelso we stop between a boarded-up tavern/apartment of dirty brick and a weedy lot by the Amtrak station. The four disembark immediately for another smoke. Leaving, we pass the city offices and the Sports Broiler, which is for sale.

The trees are darker now, more coniferous, the gold grass greened by recent rain. The bus is quieter. We are waved through at a flag stop in Castle Rock. I wonder what is turning up for the Spanish-speaking woman in the Portland bus terminal, a stranger in a strange land. I can go so many places, being anglophone and white, but for me too there are still lands, and places in my own land, where I am not comfortable or welcome. I hope she gets to the place she is seeking.

Longer odysseys have taken me to stranger places, but this one is not about distance or strangeness. For the first time in a long while I am traveling on the surface of the planet exclusively, to feel the surface and what it holds, both the spreading imprint of humankind, the opposing force of conservation, the primordial force of the earth itself, and the compromises each enforces on the other.

5

Many trips whisk the traveler from one spot to the other unaware of anything in between, muffled by jet whine and in-flight movies and peanuts and seldom a look at the ground. And that only if the cabin crew permitted the windows to be opened during the show, arrogantly unaware that the real show was outside in the face of the land and the ocean, and the cloud tops and canyons, the lines, circles and squares of *Homo sapiens* and the fractals of mountain formation, erosion, snowfall, coastline and riverine vectors.

Fourteen hours, more or less, I have flown New York to Tokyo, Anchorage to Hong Kong, Sydney to Los Angeles, Geneva to Colombo, L.A. to Helsinki, L.A. again to Auckland, Miami to Cape Town., L.A. to Buenos Aires. Breathtaking leaps around the curvature of the earth, across physical and human geography. And each time, a need to get there right away, to get on with something.

This time the experience will be tactile, never to be out of touch with the rotating tire, steel wheel, or hull that meets the surface of the planet. Except for brief instances of being airborne in mid stride on a trail. I will expend most of the variety in mode-of-travel on the outbound journey, reach the farthest point from home midway through a marathon, then roll back to where I started in one two thousand–mile bus trip that is likely to become a marathon in itself.

At Fort Lewis the bus comes in on 41st Division Drive past an airport with buff, short-cropped grass margins, squat dark helicopters in rows. One helicopter is settling into the tarmac as we roll slowly past. All non–Fort Lewis passengers must stay on the bus. Behind us is a shiny football stadium with aluminum stands, artificial turf, and a brick-colored synthetic track. Across is the Welcome and Farewell Center. At the entrance to the airport a larger-than-life soldier in bronze stands confidently with left foot atop a pile of rocks, right hand holding an automatic rifle with fixed bayonet high above his head and left hand extended, exhorting a charge towards the bus terminal.

Approaching Tacoma between walls of exurban shopping pla-zas like sclerotic plaque, the artery of traffic slows to a murky grind. Faded, decades-old signs on a brick warehouse announce Harmon Furniture Co., Hunt & Mott Wholesale, Bone Dry Shoe Co., and American Plumbing.

From the dingy, cramped Seattle terminal a three-block walk reaches Alfie's Deli and Store, where an elderly woman is obvi-ously new at making sandwiches but makes me a good turkey one, cheaper and better than Greyhound café fare. By now it is a spring-like day and except for lugging the luggage I am feeling bright and optimistic. A young woman at the coffee stand indig-nantly relates how some male didn't acknowledge that she was pregnant...at nine months. "Did he think I was just fat?"

It occurs to me that it was a difficult spot for him too...what if he assumed she was pregnant and was wrong? She concedes the point. The coffee in Seattle is as good as at home...I'd like to know what kind of coffee lies ahead.

I'm also getting somewhat anxious about checking onto the *Matanuska* in Bellingham. My ticket is only for deck passage. The word is that you can set up or sleep in a variety of places aboard, indoors or out. I'll want a good spot to call home, but how will I know what's good?

Quite a number on my bus are obviously bound for the ferry – two young women, one man on a train odyssey from South Carolina, and at least half a dozen middle-aged women in ones and twos. The excitement builds as we near Bellingham. One town to go, and a freight train blocks the road for about five minutes both going into and out of town. LPG tank cars and South Dakota Soybeans.

The train rolls on and the bus rolls down through a forest of evergreens to the shores of Puget Sound at Fairhaven, the outskirts of Bellingham. A combination bus and Amtrak station and Alaska Ferry Terminal flies the blue flag of Alaska, its Big Dipper pointing to the North Star. Nearly everyone gets off the bus here. We queue up for our tickets, then sit in line upstairs for most of the rest of the hour from three to four o'clock and then it is time to board. People stream across the gangway. A troop of twelve or so boy scouts are pitching tents and lugging big boxes of food onto the open space on the back deck where tents are being erected, duct-taped to the wooden planking. Others stake out spaces one deck higher, under a roof of yellow glass called the solarium. The forward lounge downstairs has a comfortable, spacious living-room atmosphere, but placement of personal gear there is prohibited in order to maintain access for all. The recliner lounge upstairs is old, dark and cushy with TVs in two corners. I choose the recliner lounge, starboard side (where the glacier views might be), leave my gear across two seats and go back ashore for a last run on land before the ship leaves.

It's reassuring to run for thirty minutes, even in a strange town. Touristy shops, a hill, a ballfield in a park. I watch the time carefully, taking a few turns around a park overlooking the sound. Then the return run quickly downhill, not to home but onward. To the ferry terminal, back across the gangway, and up to the recliner lounge of the *Matanuska*, home for the next four days.

II

At six o'clock (on shipboard it is five o'clock, Alaska time from here on) we slip away from the pier and head out on water that is glassy smooth, into a clear evening with wispy high clouds. Children run around the decks, excited. People gradually pull away from the front decks as the wind picks up. A few seals in the water, birds crossing overhead.

Vancouver, British Columbia, gradually slips up on the right. Island profiles overlap in the distance, like waves in the sunset in the west. Announcements are made about lifeboats, itinerary, possible whales, cafeteria schedules. Everything is amazingly tranquil, and will remain so, at least until we hit Queen Charlotte Sound in the morning. Chili is $2.75 in the cafeteria and very solid fare. I've been up since four o'clock a.m. (three o'clock

Alaska time), and since we are on a broad stretch of water with little to watch except land dimly gray in the twilight I will sleep early and happily.

The lounge carpet is just soft enough to be congenial for sleeping. The huge diesels of the ship are built to run efficiently for long distances, and warm to the task. Their purr is comforting, even up here on deck 7, and sends me right off to dreamland.

By four the next morning it is getting light and I'm awake after seven hours. We are in narrows towards the northern end of Vancouver Island, passing between high slopes with a few visible snowy patches on the left and lower, much-logged slopes on the right. Occasional clear-cuts can be seen on the steeper slopes of the island side, with one or two buildings suggesting that they can be approached by road. Here and there, the slopes break up into smaller hills, punctuated by scattered outfalls of water and rocks.

Several dozen fishing craft are on the water this morning, an occasional lodge visible on shore. Suddenly four or five black dorsal fins appear in the water dead ahead, bringing a rush of early-rising passengers to the rail. Orcas. The *Matanuska* cuts the engines way back as we slowly idle past, watching for the next emergence of black and white. Two or three different pods of four to seven animals pass, heading south, each with one large fin and a family of smaller fins alongside. For a while they seem to turn and swim alongside us, staying near the surface. Gulls, smaller birds, and one bald eagle wheel around the orcas in clouds.

After maybe thirty minutes the orcas are gone except for two stragglers far off to one side. No cabin announcement was made – you had to be up on deck at a quarter to six to see the activity of orcas, sea birds, eagles, and humans in the fish-rich narrows.

Shortly after we leave the orcas the engines rev up, and rain is tangible in the air. We are approaching the open water of Queen Charlotte Sound. A cabin announcement warns of ocean swells, seasickness. We reach the sound at nine-thirty, by which time it is very foggy and raining steadily. The swells, however, are quite gentle. I spend the morning reading, an armchair traveler except that my armchair is also traveling.

Edward Hoagland, in the volume *The Great Land*, relates that most people who journey to Alaska are in some way either escaping from an awful situation they wish to leave behind, or simply wool-gathering or self-recruiting.

I have no desire to permanently leave home, but I can see that all three do apply to me. Home ties bind but also constrain life to narrow channels of sameness. A piece of my character needs a home, another piece is restless. Runs in the forest or along the river, most weeks, can stave off the ignition of the instinct to blow town. This time, the soul said it was time to see what is on the horizon. It may have appeared self-destructive to some in my family, but I know that self-preservation is heavily involved and fighting to come out on top. Certain of my fellow passengers here too wear expressions that clearly suggest the same. Three young women, independent of each other, tending to wear knit hats and flowing cotton skirts and sandals, were in separate perches on life jacket boxes on the lee side of the boat last night, all writing in the same size spiral notebook (smaller than mine). Other passengers, male and female, angry or independent, or seeking, wear also the same do-not-attempt-to-interact-with-me look. This is not the Love Boat, unless we are united by our individual self-love, reaching away towards something distant, natural, challenging, purifying, slightly desperate in our hope for fulfillment.

Journeys are made every day to lands that are unremarkable in themselves and ordinary to their natives. Journeys of duty, cargo runs in the same narrow tidal channels of life that I had at home. The same journey, though, can be an epiphany if the conditions are right. The destination can be a paradise of fulfillment or a hell-hole of captivity, depending on one's reasons for being there, who is encountered, and the way one's internal tides are running. The selfsame town can appear to be a distant and worthy destination to a romantic traveler like me but there is always the irony that somebody in that fondest destination would be happier in the situation that I left to go there.

With the ship fogged in like this, rain dripping from every rail and sloshing on the decks, the landforms pass by unseen. The few visible aspects of the fjord country scenery are not nearly as promising as the sights of last night or early this morning. Videos play in the recliner lounge, on wildlife, the building of the ferry *Malaspina*, the blowing up of Ripple Rock (in the channel we passed during the night). People play Monopoly, cribbage, bridge, chess, in the forward lounge. A guy fiddles with his cell phone, which doesn't work here. The German honeymoon couples (there seem to be at least three) are not to be seen. Retiree-aged passengers sit and gaze from the forward windows. Tenters avoid their wet tents, walk around the ship or huddle under the solarium roof. There is no sense of escape from anywhere – we are too closed in. Wool-gathering? Too little stimulation to drown out the normal sounds of a racking brain. Self-recruitment? Harder to be as excited about your own possibilities as it was under the cirrus sunset of last evening with the last outpost of urbanness, Vancouver, dim in the haze to the east and falling astern as the moon climbed high over the layers of mountain ridges and the channels of the San Juan Islands.

Still, I meant for a part of this journey to be made within, and this is a good time to acknowledge that, to run a few laps around my inner track. A journey to a place wild and far away is a romantic concept and there is clearly in me something that turns to romance every so often and is painfully depressed in its absence. I must go down to the sea again, to the long air lanes or the open road. And every time, I partake of the experience from the start, anticipating, planning, rehearsing, even training for the journey, then joining with it as it comes to me, out of an emotional drive that is spent with the effort of travel.

I have been a runner for over thirty years. Others may have been champions, still others may be independent souls who find races artificial and prefer just to run on their own. I am in neither of these groups. An event, long or short, local or famous, is to me an opportunity to perform if only for myself, to plan, prepare, perform, and then to place in the memory. The effort is spent when the finish line is reached, if not before. The similarity between running and journeying, in these terms, has seemed as obvious and natural as breathing, for as long as I can remember. Far from being self-centered, running and journeying to me are almost the ultimate in outwardly directed experience. I come away from either with far more in tangible gain than the muscle memory of the experience and the coincidental photographs and knickknacks. A book bag is part of every running journey I have taken, at least the ones related to marathons. Each journey is the kernel of a learning process. If you aren't having fun on a journey, or a run, you aren't learning. The trick is to discover what can be learned.

The books in my bag are all from the public library, brought to this journey in hopes of taking something more away from it. John McPhee's book of essays on Alaska, *Coming Into the Country*, was once read aloud on NPR's "Books by Radio" and starts with a chapter called "What They Were Looking For." Re-reading it takes up part of my rainy morning. The diesels purr, pushing us northward. McPhee describes people of the north, and some of these are on the *Matanuska* today. Going to the Great North in search of something, or simply going home. Riding together with first-timers like me, along a string of coastal settlements with permanent residents, economies, schools, at least a few miles of road, and now even websites of their own. Human habitation in all sorts of phases, native lands and settlements, homesteads, fishing camps, tent sites. Places where these have metamorphosed into villages with electricity and water, municipal wharves, airstrips. Areas dominated by extraction industries that haul and chop logs or fish, toss the waste, or, if necessary or advantageous, process it. Areas dominated by the expedition industry, serving the needs of outsiders to plunge into the primordial purity of the northern woods and waters, if only for a few days or weeks, to strip the corrosion of civilization from the modern mind and perhaps to reach the interior lakes and campsites of their own minds.

At least one place, Sitka, was reached by the hand of humanity from another direction long before Seward's Folly imposed an American touch on these shorelines. Russian culture is still a presence there. And one other place – Juneau – has a full-blown case of civilization contracted from the outside. The symptoms include executive hotels, law offices, bureaucrats, condominia, and a government created largely by taking a rib from the governments of other states thousands of miles away.

Many human beings have come into this country. A lot have left. A few have stayed, others go back seasonally. These have found something here to call home. By now, many more have been born and raised here, know no other home, and have produced their own children and grandchildren, natives of this place only because someone came seeking something. Did those seekers primarily wish just to travel and seek, or did they find what they wanted? The days ahead will bring my feet to shores where the hand of humanity still lies lightly upon the land and the scars are still visible to show what those seekers found, and did, and in what way their lives have left trails to be trod by others.

Robert W. Service is of course in my brain. You can't leave home for the Yukon without. The ship's National Forest Interpreter, Ernestine, does a whole lecture on him, reciting huge chunks of his poetry by heart to smiles and chuckles all around. "The Cremation of Sam McGee" is as familiar as anything in American literature and there's something in us that won't let it grow old. Stuff that old poem into the fire again, Ernestine, and it will sit up and grin at us and make us laugh at the cold one more time. "The Shooting of Dan McGrew" starts "A bunch of the boys were whooping it up in the Malamute Saloon..." and you are hooked again into wondering who the solitary piano player was, and who pulled the trigger when the lights went out. Was it "the lady that's known as Lou"?

The best thing Robert W. Service wrote, though, is a lesser-known homage to the land called "The Spell of the Yukon." It may be pedestrian, but I am a runner and therefore a pedestrian of the first order, and a romantic as well. Service speaks in the voice of a man no longer young, compelled to return to the land that consumed his youth. Somehow even as a high school kid this poem spoke to me, and now that I am older, even though I still have not set eyes on his land, it speaks just as loudly. He begins,

> *I wanted the gold, and I sought it,*
> *I scrabbled and mucked like a slave.*
> *Was it famine or scurvy – I fought it;*
> *I hurled my youth into a grave.*
> *I wanted the gold, and I got it –*
> *Came out with a fortune last fall, –*
> *Yet somehow life's not what I thought it,*
> *And somehow the gold isn't all.*

I won't quote the whole poem. You can seek it out for yourself. After all, seeking is part of the gold. But this voice of a man drawn again to a land where he nearly died as a reckless youth has talons that hold you. He was looking for something too.

> *You come to get rich (damned good reason);*
> *You feel like an exile at first;*
> *You hate it like hell for a season,*
> *And then you are worse than the worst.*

And what he found was something else.

> *There's a land where the mountains are nameless,*
> *And the rivers all run God knows where;*
> *There are lives that are erring and aimless,*
> *And deaths that just hang by a hair;*[1]

---

[1] Robert W. Service, "The Spell of the Yukon" in *Collected Poems of Robert Service*. G. P. Putnam's Sons, 1940.

The poem could end a stanza earlier than it does. We are prepared to accept that he's headed to the Yukon once more. Then like someone who finds himself unexpectedly old and in the possession of a morsel of wisdom but uncertain as to whom to pass it on to, he addresses the air around him,

> *Yet it isn't the gold that I'm wanting*
> *So much as just finding the gold.*

And almost as an afterthought, four final lines.

> *It's the great, big, broad land 'way up yonder,*
> *It's the forests where silence has lease;*
> *It's the beauty that thrills me with wonder,*
> *It's the stillness that fills me with peace.*

Punch my ticket. That's where I'm bound.

III

Ketchikan in the rain. Two miles from the ferry terminal to town, and after thirty-six hours on the ship I need a run. Before the first ferry passengers are aboard the city bus, I'm briskly down the gangway in my running shoes and half a mile away down the sidewalk past the General Hospital and Utilities Board. Float planes roar overhead, trucks splash past on the main road. Industrial yard entrances to my right, steep hills to my left. The town is four miles long and seems four blocks (at most) deep. Here and there a detour is required around a forklift or a truck parked in the way. Near the city center I veer through a tunnel carved for the landward lane of traffic, where the seaward side skirts a headland. It's 7:15 and we have to be aboard by 9:00. Time to walk around, photograph the rain gauge, climb to an elevated parking lot looking over the town, find the first open coffee shop (and rest room). The morning newspaper describes a crime that

15

occurred several weeks ago on the *Matanuska*, apparently several weeks before, a rape case where the crime occurred in Canadian waters (where we have been for most of the trip so far) and yet apparently Alaska has no prosecutorial right. The offender is being held under bond in Ketchikan pending appeal, a twenty-nine-year old man. The victim was underage, sixteen. Ugly story. One would think that Alaskan law enforcement would have this one worked out by now. In the old days it probably would have been settled by rougher justice, but which way?

Ketchikan is gritty, rainy, hectic, rusty, a growling diesel engine at work. The Tongass National Forest Interpretive Center is open at 8:00 a.m., an oasis of quiet and clean comfort. Beautifully done, life-size dioramas, walk-through scenes, convincing exhibits of native survival skills. At the bookshop a worker is grousing about the building. She thinks it's so badly planned, can't believe it won a design award! I'll stay out of that subject. She also grouses about getting wet in the rain...clearly this is out of place for anyone living in Ketchikan. But when I ask, she asserts that she is from Alaska. A large quantity of free maps available, the slide show is good, and suddenly it is 8:45. I have fifteen minutes to run the two miles back to the ferry. I make it aboard in fourteen and a half, and the *Matanuska* is off northward again.

By late morning lighter patches of sky are visible. Forested mountains flank the broad channel between island and mainland Alaska. It's high-energy time on board and kids run around and around the deck while teenagers play board games and adults chatter. Winds still gust outside but the rain is slackening and it's fun viewing the waters and woods and peaks. The few signs of animal life are a couple of porpoise backs, quickly gone, and two bald eagles far off on a tree.

Wrangell will be the next stop, a town on an island across from a garnet ledge that the last owner willed to the children of Wrangell – and the kids now run the store. As young as eight, they are set up at card tables when we arrive in the early afternoon, with beautiful naturally faceted garnets priced from one to fifty dollars, many in the original matrix.

We have only an hour in Wrangell – time to stroll the town and look for a couple of souvenir shops. One is going out of business – really – and everything is cheap. The owner says he is related to the founder of Doernbecher Children's Hospital in Oregon and remembered living in posh style in Portland as a young boy, but returned to Wrangell to live. There is a small cruise ship anchored on the other side of the town, high and white. He claims it has seven hundred passengers.

I can see why this shop owner came back to Wrangell, a homey quiet place where kids ride bikes on Main Street and the gardens and homes look much like a small Oregon town. You could leave your door unlocked here, and drop in on your neighbor for coffee anytime. A few souvenir shops on the main street but otherwise it's normal, meaning you could walk in off the ferry and get a haircut as easily as a postcard. We are "pumping cash into the local economy" as they say. I do feel like a money pump, but a minuscule one compared to that sleek white cruise ship registered in Panama. It turns out that shops are required to pay rebates to the cruise lines for sales to cruise passengers. We from the *Matanuska*, besides being budget-level travelers, do not impose such burdens. I walk a couple of back streets, where geraniums grow in the yards and baking smells waft from one window, and then it's time to get back on board. Wrangell would be a nice place to live.

We've been told about the passage called the Wrangell Narrows, which we will follow between here and Petersburg. It has sixty navigational aids, and ninety course corrections in twenty miles, is only nineteen feet deep in places, and less than a hundred yards wide. For comparison, our ship draws about fifteen feet of water. As we cast off from Wrangell, the shore hand says the *Kennicott*, another state ferry, left Petersburg at 3:45 coming south. It is now 4:00, and we are going north. We will have to pass the *Kennicott* in the Narrows.

The first hour takes us back out of the wide bay on which Wrangell lies. Gradually we approach a sizable mountain on the west side, pass by it and then head for a small opening that looks like a river. The ship slows, enters the opening, and then negotiates a couple of bends as the channel narrows to something resembling a small river like the middle Willamette in Oregon but with flat, marshy banks. Big tall channel markers rise on stakes from the marsh, confining traffic to a channel not much wider than our ship. Cabins in all stages of construction and repair can be seen on either bank. The family at the first cabin is out to watch us, waving and even lighting a string of firecrackers. The ship answers with a tremendous horn blast. The echoes resound for a long time. More cabin owners wave, more horn blasts answer. Someone on shore moons the ship, and everybody on board and ashore laughs. The passengers on the *Matanuska* are out on the deck in numbers as the ship steers around the tight corners in the channel. It seems impossible that this channel could lead again to open ocean, very possible that we could wind up at the head of a creek somewhere in the hills ahead. Suddenly around a bend we see, perhaps half a mile away, another white and blue ship, ridiculously large in the small channel. The *Kennicott*.

We pull to the right in front of a channel marker, and cut our engines way back while the *Kennicott* squeezes past to general waving and cheering from the decks on both ships. We are no more than twenty yards apart, rail to rail. Then the *Matanuska* revs the diesels and turns hard to port, almost at a right angle, rounding the marker on the proper side to get back in the channel again. The tide must be flowing against us to give us that much steering power.

Everyone stays on deck as we continue the spectacular passage through the Narrows. More houses line both sides, some built on homestead claims and others on lots won in public land lotteries. Many of these places are accessed by water from Petersburg at the north end of the Narrows, though here and there a gravel road is visible. Clouds thicken again, though no rain is falling as the channel starts to broaden into a smooth dark passage. Below decks for a moment, I mention to a man working in the galley that we have passed the other ferry. He shakes his head. His brother is working on the *Kennicott* and he's been trying to reach him on the phone for a week, but had no idea the two ships were passing each other in the Narrows.

Petersburg is a prosperous fishing town with several operating canneries, though we really don't have any time to see it, just thirty minutes to stretch our legs on shore. It's a Norwegian town with Nordic Drive intersecting Hansen Street. Later afternoon is changing to evening, and there's little to do here but take a few photos with the aperture wide open, hoping for the best. From the deck as we depart my binoculars can see into the canneries, where men and women in rubber rain gear sort fish on processing lines, flinging salmon on down towards the machinery that will send them to grocery shelves in faraway towns.

Thursday is coming to an end and it has been as tiring as Wednesday was confining. I'm finding the soup and chili in the cafeteria are all I need to survive, along with the trail mix and energy bars I brought in quantity. This is the third night on shipboard, and I go to sleep before 9:00, hoping to get a sight of the Sitka Narrows early in the morning.

IV

A blast of the ship's horn at 5:45. We are in patches of heavy fog, negotiating a series of channels that would seem quite narrow except for our experience in the Wrangell Narrows the day before, which stretched belief. The water here is smooth and mirror-like, and the channel veers widely to left and right through small forested islands, here and there opening to broad lake-like areas. Fishing boats stream past us single file as the sky lightens, and visibility varies from excellent to zero as we cruise through and between fog patches. It makes good watching.

The Sitka ferry terminal is seven miles from town, too far for a runner who also wants to see the sights. There is a round trip shuttle on an old school bus. Sitka is situated in a strikingly beautiful bay dotted with pine wooded islands (and this morning containing three cruise ships). Little is open at 7:00 but we walk around – up on the bridge to Japonskii Island, the site of the old Russian fort, the main street. Everything is close together. The Tlingit Cultural Center and Centennial Center promise dance shows at 9:30 and 10:30 (Tlingit and Russian, respectively), but we will have to be gone by 8:30. The town economy is timed to the cruise ships. By 8:00 cruise passengers start to arrive and predictably, shops start to open. On the way back to the bus I find that the old Orthodox Church is open. The inside is stunning. Here are gilt ornaments and bibles that might have arrived when Baranof was governor, around 1790. All of these icons and ornaments were heroically saved from a fire in the 1950s and the current wooden structure dates from then, but the scent of incense and the flicker of candles evoke the traditions of centuries. The church interior must be really impressive in the long winter dark. Just enough time remains to drink in the sight of the ancient icons and two bearded priests in their black vestments inside. It is still a large, working church, and clearly still a very Russian town in history and tradition. The bus leaves in five minutes.

The *Matanuska* is away by 9:00, back through the Sitka Narrows on the same course we traveled in the small hours of the morning. As the channel widens, it is high-energy time on board again. Three hundred eleven passengers are aboard, the most so far, and the car deck is full. We see deer on shore, a dozen or more bald eagles, seals lying on low gravelly islands, and finally whales off at a distance in a mirror-still reach of water before we re-enter the main passage

I haven't written about the moment-to-moment business of ship life, spotting birds, watching water traffic, kids running around. Talks by Ernestine the National Forest Interpreter, the films upstairs for entertainment, car-deck calls for people to walk their pets (and clean up after them). Bored people sit in the bar or play solitaire while very terrain-focused people like me are always outside. A lot can be seen from the deck of a ship. Logging cuts, old and new, are infrequent but conspicuous. One particularly horrendous example is on Admiralty Island, starboard side going north towards Juneau. It belongs to a native corporation, according to Ernestine, and has been an ongoing clear-cut for 25 years. There is a small mill at the waterfront, and stockpiles of logs. Regulating cutting in the Tongass will have to mean regulating outfits like this – politics and all. Most cuts are small enough to seem swallowed up in the vastness of the Tongass, but this cut is miles long and shows very little evidence of regeneration. According to the NF center in Ketchikan, little is done to replant after the Tongass is logged – the theory is natural regeneration. The smaller cuts we have seen do show some evidence of regeneration but the big ones according to Ernestine don't seem to show the growth you would expect for their age. She says this slowly and very tactfully, with a slight smile. The stress of politics in the forestry business here must be enormous. The potential riches certainly are. I have seen no sign of selective cutting.

Being vigilant on-deck brings two more whale sightings. In this wide passage, though, each is more than a mile away. And both are attended by watchers in small boats, despite the law against pursuit. The ferry does not slow to give these whales room as it did with the orcas on the first morning – they are simply too far off. There is considerable boat traffic as we make a U-turn south into a different passage for Juneau. Now huge glaciers are in the mountains to the west, mute blue-white tongues of ice and cold, their crevasses visible miles out to sea.

The state ferry docks thirteen miles from Juneau. There is no bus or shuttle into the state capital. Thirteen miles from town, and the state wants you to pay city taxi rates. Even the city bus comes no nearer than two miles. This is nuts. With a few others, I decide Juneau isn't worth the cost. Instead, we split the cost of a taxi ride up to the Mendenhall Glacier. On the way we drop off a father and son who live in the valley below the glacier in a new development of big houses. For their sake I hope the glacier doesn't reverse its recent trend and begin to advance – they are only about five miles below it. The glacier ends in a beautiful lake with floating bits of ice in it. I have enough time for a jog alongside this arctic landscape, and enough film for a couple of snapshots. Then it's back to the ship for a shower and a salad.

As we slip out of Juneau in the gathering evening I sit alone in the forward lounge room watching a few gaps in the clouds reflect the long northern twilight. Someone is setting off fireworks from a nearby island, the flicker of a campfire still visible through binoculars. It is the last night on the ship. We will be in Skagway before dawn.

V

Five hours of sleep are surprisingly refreshing. At Skagway it is warm in the predawn and there is no wind. I walk the half mile to town at three-thirty and sit in a small park by the rail depot, near a statue of a Tlingit guide and a young prospector facing off towards the pass, the Tlingit's arm extended.

What they were looking for here is obvious. The current character of a place is shaped by the work of those who stayed to work. In Ketchikan it's industry. In Wrangell it's fishing and outdoor expedition outfitting, in Petersburg it is canneries. Sitka began with Russian territorial ambitions. Juneau is government, United States style. Skagway and nearby Dyea, now a ghost town, were not the gold fields themselves, but the gateway. The Canadian authorities at the border knew how little infrastructure there was in the Yukon and correctly anticipated that thousands of young men would hurl their youth into the grave in pursuit of gold in a land that could not cope with their most basic demands for necessities. Each of the sourdoughs bound for the Yukon had to haul two thousand pounds of food and supplies to the Canadian border at the top of the pass in order to cross into the territory. Men formed partnerships, cooperated or fought, struggled up the passes over and over again building their caches of supplies at the top, then crossed the alpine high country and floated down the Yukon to Dawson or the Klondike, often to find that the best claims were already taken.

By four-thirty it is light enough to read (and write) and listen to the creek. By four-fifty a light mist is falling but the sky is lightening rapidly. Time to stash the bags and loosen up the legs. The town has a restored, theme-park look. Running up Main Street in Skagway brings me past the original cabin of one William Moore, who settled here ten years prior to the rush. His dream of profitably controlling access to the pass was ignored and overrun by the first wave of stampeders. The Tlingit too must have watched, or been muscled aside, exploited and infected, or may even have profited doing Sherpa service but even then been altered forever by the exposure to cash economy. Just as most of the stampeders did not get rich in anything except experience. Cash aside – and you can't take that with you – are we any better today?

Well, you can take it with you electronically, at least as far as Skagway, which provides a cash machine and a phone for a call home where all is well. They seem to understand that Dad's just out running. A cold drizzle begins to fall. The snow patches on the high mountainsides of the fjord shine through the grayness. Several of the Skagway buildings are on closer inspection original, identifiable from old photographs displayed in the windows. As eight o'clock approaches, scores of tourists materialize. Yes, a cruise ship has just docked.

An old wood-burning pufferbelly backs into a railroad siding, flames in the firebox and black soot streaming, and connects to three old passenger cars. On a second track, two aged-looking diesel units are hooked up to six or seven more cars. It turns out that more than forty cars are in the yards, restored and purchased from narrow-gauge railways all over the world. More than just a tourist-trap operation, the White Pass & Yukon Railway actually continued to haul ore all the way from Whitehorse as recently as the 1980s. I am seated in the only car marked "independent travelers" as we pull out of the Skagway terminal and along the creek beside the cemetery. Past the graves of Soapy Smith and of Frank Reid, the "town hero" who shot Soapy in a duel, the only problem being that Soapy also shot Frank.

The White Pass & Yukon was built in two years during a depression by thirty-five thousand men, with "only" thirty-five casualties. We see a cross commemorating two of them, on a huge slab of granite that crushed the men and their animals after a blast. After this the grade becomes really steep, 3.9% out of a theoretical maximum of 4%. The forest changes from mixed deciduous (aspen, alder, bigleaf maple) to subalpine fir and we are soon in hazy mist. The trestles are dizzying and the track clings to one precipice after another. Crossing the pass brings a moonscape of lichen and stunted firs, potholes of water, and ghostly telephone poles without wires.

The border post of Fraser, British Columbia, is a dividing point. The train now goes no farther. A dozen of us "independents" disembark and are transferred to a bus going on to Whitehorse. Everybody else goes back to Skagway on the train. For the next two hours the bus winds down, first through the moonscape and then along long lakes and subalpine country. The town of Carcross is a few buildings huddled in a depression beside a lake. Abandoned mine sites by the road, rock heaps next to doors into the earth. The Carcross Desert appears, incongruous amid the gray and green rocks and lakes. The landscape is both haunting and forbidding, vast and cool even in August. Few of those who came here have stayed. Perhaps as many live off the needs of the traveler as off the bounty of the land, for in the long run the impetus to come to this faraway land must needs balance with the carrying capacity of the land itself. A solitary house by the road displays the sign "Eat here or we'll both starve!"

VI

As we near Whitehorse, I'm all eyes to pick out parts of the race course I will run the next morning, but the highway remains out of sight of the river until we turn in the main drive to town. I lug my duffel to the Gold Rush Inn, a comfortable if more-than-I-need Best Western, where the lobby is full of old mining gear and the elevator door is painted to look like a safe.

It's time to reconnoiter. How much time will I have to catch the bus after the race on Sunday? A lot, it turns out, because Sunday, not Monday, is the day the buses don't run. Greyhound in the U.S. had the information wrong. The good news is that I'll have all day Sunday to finish and recover, but the bad news is that I will have to leave on Monday, like it or not. That eliminates the possibility of having to run for the bus after the race, but also the possibility of getting home Tuesday night.

Whitehorse offers a museum, also the No-Pop Sandwich Shop, several large government buildings, an airport on the bluff above the river, a good bookstore (Fireweed) and the promise of more. I will explore more on Sunday afternoon and Monday morning. Now it's time for a nap and a pasta dinner and to get off my feet. I'm bursting with inactivity after days on shipboard and a long morning on the train and bus. It will feel good to run tomorrow, but for now it will be better to keep it bottled up.

As an added bonus, the Track & Field World Championships are on both U.S. and Canadian TV. The Canadian channels show more running and far less chitchat. The live feed is on the French channel. This is further inspiration for running, and I watch several events. It is raining off and on, sometimes quite hard.

That evening in the restaurant I can overhear five prospectors sharing stories over beer. So present-day Whitehorse apparently still has authentic Yukon moments. I listen more closely. The most vocal of them gripes that his son majored in geology at "the university," then tried to tell him there was no soapstone in a particular valley.

"So who the hell do ya think has been mining soapstone there for the last twenty years? These kids, they don't know nothing." The speaker would look perfect with a pick and shovel and gold pan. And giving him a jackass would make two of a kind.

Outside, it stays light enough to read until after 10:00 p.m. this August 4.

VII

Sunday, race day. A little walking around discloses a Tim Horton's Donuts with coffee and muffins. Walking down to the race area at seven-fifteen I am the only one there. Then it's seven-thirty. The start is set for eight, and according to the map this is the place. Two other runners show up, as puzzled as I am. Finally, minutes before eight six or seven cars appear and rapidly, efficiently, disgorge timing and finish line equipment, tents, refreshments, registration tables, the works. It's cool (good) and quite humid (not good) and a T-shirt seems to be the right choice to race in. I choose the gray poly fiber shirt I ran in at Ketchikan. It smells not so good but that is of little importance. After four hours of running it will smell a lot worse.

The Yukon itself would qualify as a river that "runs God knows where." The river rises barely fifty miles from the ocean in the glacier fields, then flows inland. At Whitehorse it courses between clay cliffs, blue and rushing away towards the northern horizon. The sourdoughs rode this river to the gold fields of the Klondike further north but the journey of this mighty river is not nearly finished there. If you throw a wood chip into the current at Whitehorse it will eventually make its way to Nome and then out into the Bering Strait, two thousand miles away.

The Yukon River Trail Marathon is a full marathon in length, twenty-six miles three hundred eighty-five yards and probably a little more for good measure, nearly all on dirt cross-country ski trails along the Yukon below the town. The race is also divided into four sections of increasing length and difficulty to accommodate those who run it as two- and four-runner teams.

The starter has the ninety or so runners assemble at a line on the park path, hushes us for final instructions, and then gets tongue-tied. A bear was spotted on the course the day before. "If you see a bear, uh…wait for another…" (Another what, bear?) Then the starter says go, as starters must do. The small group of runners heads out. Past the old steamboat *Klondike*, now a historic relic sitting high and dry at the end of the park. The pack quickly strings out as the trail forces us into a single file part way up the steep right bank of the Yukon. With so few runners in the race most soon are running alone, northward under the blowing gray skies, eyes on the trail footing and the runner in sight ahead. As in life, few of us ever seem to look at the string of runners behind.

It feels wonderful to run again, glorious to have all day to do it. Bus, boat, train, the means to this end, feet now pushing against gravity, striding above a path as they were meant to do, mooting questions of running from self, from home. Just running. So far from home, yet doing something so familiar. The day invites comparisons of size and distance. One runner is a very small animal, a tiny mote less than two meters high on the surface of a very large planet. I came perhaps a thousand miles. Twenty-six miles is short compared to that. Yet twenty-six miles is roughly twenty-six thousand strides. It is also five times the height of Everest. So large, so small. The river flowing beside us on its own long journey.

After six miles the course crosses over a picturesque wooden suspension bridge between the steep narrows of Miles Canyon. Postcards I saw in the hotel show the *Klondike* steaming through this canyon as serious, bowler-hatted young men with moustaches stand on the decks. Perhaps those very men had personally lugged 2,000 pounds of gear over the Chilkoot or White Pass to get there and now were on their way to the gold fields to see whether their dreams could be sustained.

At the suspension bridge the first stage ends. Relay teams change runners here but we marathoners just keep going. From here the happily soft and springy trail leads farther downriver through a variety of forest environments, along cross-country ski trails, past lakes and through lovely green scenery that in general just doesn't quit. The rain has kept the dust down, and the cloud cover is just enough to keep the temperature cool without making the day gloomy. I am in that happy equilibrium where breathing, running, observing and thinking come naturally, each activity giving and taking life from the others. Fatigue is still an hour or two off in the future.

In a low forested area around mile ten, a simple sign notes that we are in the former site of Canyon City, once a boat landing and river town on the Yukon below Whitehorse and Miles Canyon. This point is also the farthest I will be from home on my journey. Appropriately, for I am running right down the former Front Street and past the site of the landing area, once a bustling hub of stores and houses, in the very steps of thousands who came to escape or discover or get far away from something or closer to something else. None of that remains, and if any of them are still alive they have gone. In a few hundred strides I too will be gone. Southward.

We are zipping through a still pine forest following a chocolate brown path under silent trees, through chokecherries and willows. I have a cardboard camera in my pocket, taking snapshots. It's something I wish I had done more in other races, and this one has scenery. There is good support with eight feed-and-water stations that materialize out of the forest just as one is about to give up all hope. After the first miles I am running mostly alone, with other runners often in sight but not within conversation range. At one point I find that the runner ahead of me wears a T-shirt saying *South Pole Station*, clearly someone I have to talk to. I learn that he leaves the Yukon in winter for the sunnier clime of the high Antarctic summer, where he operates meteorological equipment. We share stories of Antarctic travels.

Stages two and three offer mile after pretty mile of trail through woods, along lake and river margins. A couple of hills near the end of stage three force a slower pace. The Lions Club is staffing the food and exchange station at the end of stage three and they give me a rousing cheer as I approach. By way of salute I take a snapshot of them all with my cardboard camera.

Then in the fourth quarter of the race come four more hills, difficult ones, the last one guaranteed to cramp anybody's tired legs. This is also where marathon runners, at least on roads, often "hit the wall," expending all energy resources and slowing to a characteristic stagger. One advantage of trail running, however, is that the constant change in footing requires the runner to use many different muscles and gaits. Trail runners also tend to run more slowly and eat as we run, and therein lies the key to not hitting the wall. We can balance the equation by taking in more food, keeping the glucose higher, and thereby maintaining energy for longer. I have been eating energy food at each of the stops, but the final hill kills my legs thoroughly. The result is a painful walk uphill in the soft sandy soil. For me, this race is not about time, however, and walking a few hundred yards at a time in a trail race is fairly normal. Then we are out of the trails and nearing town, and the legs return to life though each step demands effort and exacts a promise that the end will occur. The last miles of the course return to town along the rapids of the Yukon, rushing like white horses' manes (hence the name) through a reach of river fitted with kayak slalom "gates" suspended over the rapids on wires for serious modern-day whitewater paddling competitions. Then over a bridge and then to the city park again. Wet clouds still blanket the cool midday. A few yards from the end of the race, I remember to pull out the camera again and coolly take a picture of the finish line.

The race director said to add an hour to your road-marathon time because of the terrain and use that as a target for this race. Well, at 4:25 maybe I'm not so slow after all, although forty-five minutes would probably be a better correction factor. The men's winner is 3:10, women's 3:36. I'm about twenty-second out of fifty-six marathoners, and in this small race I am second in my age group, which gets me a certificate. The finisher's medals for those of us who came as romantic journey-takers should probably be made of fool's gold but in fact are ceramic, fired from local Yukon River clay and threaded on white and red maple-leaf ribbons.

There is a summery post-race barbecue under white tents. Anvil-like thunderheads hang downstream in late afternoon sun that yellows the clay cliffs on either side of the river. Awards are handed out and runners can mingle. I meet several locals and others from around Canada. One runner had intended this race to complete his cycle of marathons in all 50 U.S. states and all Canadian provinces, only to learn that a new territory, Nunavut, has just been created. Undaunted, he has just vowed to go to a race there at Yellowknife in only a few weeks! A very athletic looking woman runner has just returned from the Antarctic Marathon where, this year, conditions were too harsh for the runners to land. Not to be denied, she and several others charted a hundred-meter circuit around the ship's deck and ran it…four hundred twenty-two times…to equal the required distance. I share my story of having done the same race in 1997, on land more or less as planned. I feel rather guilty at her expressions of envy. The year I went our party was able to make landings at thirteen locations compared to only one or two for her. Antarctica is still a good trip, she agrees.

VIII

Monday, up early for a list of last-minute things to do. Coffee at the No-Pop, books at Fireweed, photos of things I want to remember. Two Harleys have been parked outside the hotel all weekend, one pulling a trailer made of a wooden wine barrel, the other a trailer made of a coffin complete with silver handles.

The mining exhibit at the museum is marvelous, both for minerals and for history, presenting a touch of life in the old-time camps as well as current prospecting objectives. Another museum feature is the cabin of the real Sam McGee, a prospector and friend of Robert Service, who used McGee's name in the ballad. The poem notwithstanding, the exhibit explains that Sam

McGee was actually from Peterborough, Ontario, not Tennessee, liked the cold, and lived in the cabin with his wife from 1900 to 1910, then died an old man in 1940. Service lived until 1955. I go for a short run over to the pioneer cemetery perhaps three blocks away, just to loosen up. Improbably, I sprain an ankle on a curb and walk back.

I down a sandwich for lunch and lug everything to the bus for a check-in well ahead of time. This turns out to be a good idea. Every seat is full. The bus heads out into a brightly lit afternoon and 900 miles of fireweed and fir and alder and "rivers that run God knows where," between here and Dawson Creek.

How does a journey like this one affect your ability to deal with the real world you left behind a week previously, when you stood shaking your head at the obstacles, the actualities, the relentless pursuit of demands? At first escape, one is euphoric at having left it all for a week. The first delicious steps of the trip feel as much a leap *away from* as a leap *into*. Now, as the bus speeds into the deepening afternoon, it is the winding down phase of the journey, the return to the home. Without a home, all life would be a journey without a finish line. I finished my race yesterday, now turn towards the finish at least of this longer event. Does finishing a journey provide more than the satisfaction of motion, a distance and a time – does it bring insight to knock away problems, or perspective from which to see through and around them, make them vanish? Some of this would indeed be a most welcome souvenir from a journey, even if such benefits never rise to the level of answers.

At the moment I'm in a bus with whatever life forms have boarded with me. "We all live in tide pools of one sort or another"– and a visit to a different tide pool does not in itself rid us of the essential facts of tide pool life, chief among them the fact that we must continually react to whatever else has washed in during the past twelve hours. There is more than enjoyment in chance encounter, sometimes far more.

I am seated next to a science teacher from Fort St. John who was out prospecting with his eleven-year-old son but rolled over in the 8-wheel (Argo) conveyance they were using, severely injuring himself. He has had to be flown to Whitehorse for emergency medical attention, X-rays of the orbital area, and many stitches. The boy was unharmed, is staying with acquaintances in Watson's Lake until his mother can drive up from Fort St. John, a very long way. My seatmate has a lot to be thankful for, is replaying the incident in his mind. His boy could have been out there alone with a dead father. He has come seeking minerals and in fact has lost all his samples, but found something of an entirely different nature on this trip. We have a lot to talk about including minerals, teaching in the Yukon/BC, North American tectonics, what BC kids do when they graduate, etc., etc. He is interested that I have been in the Antarctic. As with others I meet, we do not exchange names.

At Watson Lake, BC, I shoot half a dozen pictures of the stupefyingly large forest of signs, tens of thousands of signs from all over the world. Most are names of municipalities, many of these with mileages appended apparently, but not always measured from where we stand at this subarctic highway crossroads. Others are tokens of expeditions, names of passengers, family members, towns and dates. Many of these are very attractively made, obviously with tools, before departure. I heard of such a sign, made by a Canby man I met at a soccer game, and sure enough here is a Canby OR sign with five-year dates since '90, the last one only carved and not painted. Do these signs bring any new perspectives or solutions to their authors now that they are posted at Watson Lake for the notice of any and all passers-by? Did their authors' journeys contain any more value because of this? No, and yes, yes because bringing that sign here from, say, Defiance, Ohio, or Kitzbuhel, Austria, was in itself a pilgrimage, the placing of a stone in building a cathedral of travel that it might be seen by other pilgrims. It is a meta-statement about the nature of travel. What is the extent of the span of such a statement? If it should fall, will there be a sound? None of the signs is going to be here forever. The sign-posters are one step further into the performance than are those of us who merely read the signs, yet each needs the other and all, in the very near future, go on to live, love, and die in other places than Watson Lake, BC.

At Watson Lake we pick up a French bicyclist with whom I share a seat. He has bought a very cheap bike in Vancouver, fixed it up, and has ridden the Cassiar Highway (west of the normal route, up closer to the Pacific). I don't learn his name, either. Call him FB. Previously he has done the same thing in Iceland and Chile. The people in Watson Lake do not explain to him the difference between baggage and freight, however, which will create a problem the next morning in Dawson Creek." His English is quite limited and nobody attempts to communicate with him in French. He has spent six nights in Hyder, Alaska, at Misty Fjords National Park, and has seen coyotes and moose and much more from the bike. While the light lasts, I finish reading Wasa-Wasa, an eyewitness account of life in the gold fields by Harry Macfie, translated from the Swedish. The twilight lasts for two hours, the glow for another hour. Then an attempt at conversation with FB, and off to sleep until an early morning "buffet" breakfast at 5:00 at Fort Nelson, a low-ceilinged cabin with rudimentary steam tables. From there it's a four-hour haul to Dawson Creek.

By the time we reach Fort St. John we are in civilization, pastures, horses and cattle, a hay crop on the ground. One more hour and it is time to change buses in Dawson Creek, where I can amble into town past a country-western bar blaring music loud enough to be heard two blocks away, part of some kind of radio "country marathon" (we all have our favorite events), and the Full Belli Deli (sushi on Fridays) to the much-photographed zero mile marker of the Alaska Highway. I, too, photograph it much, also the gaudy Alaska Hotel across the street.

Meanwhile, back at the bus depot, FB has been absorbing lectures from Greyhound Canada people who tell him his bike is freight, not baggage, and that lack of prior preparation on his part does not constitute an emergency on theirs, etc. etc., all of which goes right over his head. I explain to him that they want to ship his bike later, not on our bus. I know that he has a flight back to Paris tomorrow. His personal belongings are wrapped up in the bike package because that's the way they did it at Watson Lake. We have thirty minutes. He pulls out an exacto knife and I help him rip off the cardboard. As maybe thirty people look on, we remove his belongings and cram them into a dirty old duffel bag (he's been on the road six weeks), then take everything off the bike that he considers worth saving – nuts, bolts, tires, tubes, generator – and squeeze it all into the duffel somehow. A young Greyhound woman adamantly tells me that he can't leave the bike, now just a frame, in front of their office. So, I locate a dumpster down the street that fortunately is empty and FB and I toss bike, wheels, cardboard, tape, and handlebars into it with three minutes to spare. I'm a bit surprised that nobody else has helped, but not at all sorry that I have. This has considerably livened up the journey. Maybe the others were a bit put off by his rather wild appearance, or by mine? Well, it's their loss. At least he will make his plane.

The six-hour trip to Prince George is utterly beautiful. Pastures of plenty, rivers, Rocky Mountain vistas, and long summer lakes. The only seat available this time is front row center next to an obese woman who takes up three-quarters of two seats, keeping her arms folded so as not to need any more space. It turns out that she is another casualty, a cook at mile four-hundred-something on the Alaska Highway who on Saturday sliced off the end of her right ring finger while cutting tomatoes. She was going home to Prince George in two weeks anyway, so is seeking medical treatment and a little rest. She will be back up on the highway in October. She is pleasant, talks about family, hasn't traveled much (Seattle) but would like to…and points out features of Prince George as we roll in around four in the afternoon. It's a very attractive, obviously prosperous place (probably meaning wood products) of seventy-eight thousand. The bus station is next to a huge new mall with a shiny new coffee shop – just the place I need to sit and get the journal up to date – plus a sub sandwich shop. Classic "home neighborhood" streets frame big lawns with dilapidated white fences, gravel alleys, spreading chestnut trees, kids and dogs in the afternoon sun. Very tranquil. I get caught up in writing the narrative, and make it back to the terminal with less than three minutes to spare.

Prince George to Vancouver is a twelve-hour run overnight. A long-golden twilight of river and mountain vista – how much great scenery can there be on a single trip – and this part of the ride is fun until it gets dark. Then the night is cramped and miserable for sleeping. The bus is less crowded but offers very little knee room in any seat and not enough lateral room to lie sideways.

Morning brings Vancouver, sparkling in clear sunshine. Passengers tumble off toward other buses. The Frenchman discovers that city buses are free today because a strike was settled yesterday, and is off to see the town and then on to the airport. One step outside the station I am panhandled by a young woman looking for change. Looking about I see at least a half dozen more young people on the square looking as though they are there for the same purpose. Big town, magnet for youth, no jobs, beg at the bus station. Being well-dressed probably helps her – the shabbier looking ones are getting ignored. I hope they get where they are going.

On the bus again, south towards the border. A retired accountant and city planner observes that many public school teachers use two to three thousand bucks of their own money for school supplies for their classes. Not surprising, but really depressing.

With an hour between buses in Seattle I return to the same deli-store that I visited on the way north and eat the same turkey sandwich but somehow it is not the same. It is later in the day, the sun is hotter, the floor has not been swept. It is also later in my life.

The local pulls out of Portland and through the Willamette Valley in the hour before sunset, golden light spilling across freshly mown hay fields, green mint and orchards. No place on the trip has looked better than this – gold at last. It feels like three or four weeks that I've been gone, very satisfying to the travel itch, but it has only been eight days off the calendar. It was certainly more about the journey than the destination. It wasn't the gold that I wanted after all, so much as the journey towards the gold. Still it is the destination that determines the journey, and thereby determines the scenery passively present along the way, and the fellow travelers who have made similar choices to take a journey in the same direction on the same path on the same day and in the same vehicle. Just like running a race, even to the fact that without a finish line to attain it is not complete.

I hardly stopped to take more than a mental snapshot of that great big bold land 'way up yonder, mostly because I had to meet a tight schedule even to make the trip at all. I was running a race, and that implies a certain amount of not stopping. Yet it was an encounter, in part with the forests where silence has lease, but also with something equally timeless. Up there is not home...home is home. And the proof of the race is in completing the course in good form, start to finish, and keeping something of it in muscle memory and something more durable in the back of one's mind. Both for future races, and for the race that is life. And that finish line will come too, and soon enough.

BOOK BAG

John McPhee, *Coming Into the Country*

Harry Macfie, *Wasa-wasa*

Robert W. Service, *The Collected Poems of Robert Service*

Asia

Traditional grave markers in the fields along a country road in northern Japan.

(photo by Nancy R. Rosenberger)

河口湖国際マラソン
Lake Kawaguchi International Marathon
Kawaguchi-ko, Japan
November 1983

Lake Kawaguchi

Kawaguchi-ko City

Start
Finish

↓ Mt. Fuji
~ 10 miles

Morioka

Tokyo

Hiroshima

Kyoto

Osaka

Lake Kawaguchi

KAWAGUCHI:

The Lake Kawaguchi International Marathon as it was run in 1983, a short loop over the bridge and back into Kawaguchi-ko town, followed by two full loops around the lake.

CHAPTER 2

Like a Guest

Lake Kawaguchi International Marathon, Japan, November 1983

> *The water is clear right through the earth,*
> *A fish goes along like a fish.*
> *The sky is vast straight into the heavens,*
> *A bird flies just like a bird.*

Dogen (1200–1253) on meditation,
after Hung-chih (1091–1157),
translation by Carl Bielefeldt[2]

PART 1, 1970–1974

I

Fresh out of college, going not to the tired capitals of Europe or the safe havens of Canada and Caribbean, but Asia where there was a war and is a war.

A teaching job, a contract, and a line to sign on. An engagement ring to a girl back home. The Boeing 707 is already high

---

[2] Translation by Carl Bielefeldt, *Dogen's Manuals of Zen Meditation.* Berkeley, University of California Press, 1988, p. 204

over the Pacific Ocean. For Japan, ancient learning and modern industry, Zen and honor, and atomic bomb ruins. Japan, where the severed head of a famous novelist has just appeared on the front page of a morning newspaper. My seatmate speaks to me in Japanese.

What are you going to Japan for?

I am trying to remember basic sentences, the polite forms of verbs, words for older and younger sister/brother, uncle, aunt, teacher.

Why do you want to go to Japan? Everything is expensive. Japan is…How much does a bottle of Johnny Walker cost where you live?

I have only a vague memory of liquor ads in the Chicago papers where I grew up, and certainly no idea of the price of any specific brand. I enjoy a beer or two after playing soccer or basketball or baseball or running, but whiskey is no part of my universe. I tell him I don't know.

Well, how much do you think it would cost? About how much?

I still don't know. And say so.

Okay, but…About how much do you think it might cost?

This conversation is going nowhere. How much does it cost in Japan, I ask.

It's incredibly expensive. They make it expensive. Over ten thousand yen. Way over.

Ten thousand yen at the time is only about twenty-six dollars. I'd get more pleasure out of twenty-six dollars' worth of a lot of things than one bottle of whatever he drinks. Does it taste better than *sake*? is the one question I know how to ask.

You have to start somewhere. Vapid it may be, but we are speaking in Japanese. We all choose the problems we work on.

II

MORIOKA, IWATE PREFECTURE

My first lodging is in an old Russian Orthodox church beside Takamatsu Pond overlooking the northern Japanese city of Morioka. There are three in the household, the Reverend, a young domestic, and myself. We are an odd combination by any standard, and I am not necessarily the oddest.

The Reverend was a Japanese prisoner in Siberia during World War II, and apparently converted to the Orthodox faith there. I spend several Sunday mornings standing through services in the cold church listening to his chanting in Russian and formal Japanese, absorbing little more than the incense. Kazuko, the young woman, has an arm and leg that are not fully developed. Her rural family has more or less abandoned her as unable to lead an adult life. She walks with a pronounced limp, and is palpably low on self-esteem. One winter afternoon she comes home with a goldfish in a bag of water, bought from a vendor at the bus station, and the next morning the fish is dead under a sheet of ice in its plastic dish. I try an expression of pity, but Kazuko laughs raucously. The dead fish seems to make her feel better.

The Reverend has Kazuko do the cooking for the three of us, coaching her on basic dishes such as powdered Knorr soup with quail eggs, braised tofu, cabbage salads, as she vacillates between moments of cheer and long disgruntled sulks. One day she is grousing about her inability to cook well, and the Reverend counters by sunnily intoning "Kazuko is nice. Kazuko can do many things. I like Kazuko." She snaps back at him, almost snarling. I see an opportunity to be funny. In the Reverend's voice I say "I *don't* like Kazuko," but I am grinning from ear to ear. This stops her snarl and leaves her puzzled as to what to do next. In a moment all three of us are laughing at the ridiculousness of it all.

Kazuko immediately brightens whenever it becomes apparent that I am even more helpless in Japanese society than she is. I feel like a goldfish in a bowl anyway, and to her a goldfish is something she can feel superior to. She often laughs uproariously at something I say or do. I speak only in basic sentences, but I can clown, and we get along very well on that basis. The three of us are a veritable comedy team as we watch television in the winter evenings, laughing together and eating mandarin oranges by the case.

At the school, I am a full-time guest teacher of English. At first, teaching means mostly leading students in pronunciation and grammar drills, but only for sixteen class hours a week. Two or three classes a day, including Saturdays. The rest of the time I spend by the hot stove in the teachers' room. Other teachers must shoulder responsibility for student evaluation and advancement, liaison with parents, curriculum, lesson coordination and more, but I have time for language learning. They must work in a rigid hierarchy, with heavy responsibilities. The schedule and school protocol are equally rigid. All school years, vacation and special days begin with ceremonies. Each morning begins with a recorded routine of warmup calisthenics, broadcast nationally over the radio at the same hour. Then there is the day's opening meeting in the teachers' room.

My relatively easy conditions cause resentment in some, because young Japanese employees normally face long hours of basic tasks for very low pay. But the freedom I have enjoyed in my education arouses curiosity. Students in Japan have college ambitions and face very difficult entrance exams. Several teachers take time to attempt conversation or to help me with Japanese, as well as to discuss anything of interest. One question that comes up time and again is whether I eat bread or rice. I like both, and say so. But that answer does not satisfy my hosts. Many of them eat both too, but this is not what is being asked. The question really means "Are you like us, are you going to become one of us, or are you basically different?" Not knowing how to answer the deeper question, I usually address the shallower one. I did not intend to move to Japan permanently, and that is probably the most honest way to put it. Some days it is all so strange, so alien to the taste for personal freedom acquired during my teen and college years, that I can hardly conceive of living permanently among so many rules.

In the city a foreigner is conspicuous, like it or not. There are perhaps five Caucasian faces among two hundred thousand residents of Morioka, meaning instant recognition by over seven hundred students or any member of their families. Every bus trip taken, every movie gone to or onion bought, might plausibly be noted by someone who knows who I am, where I work, and how I got there. The city registry even has my fingerprints and my address, as required by law.

Buses crawl on chained tires through snowy streets. More snow falls, building foot-numbing slush. The charcoal-burning stoves at school, the cups of green tea, the steaming hot bowls of rice help to fight the damp cold. Best of all, though, are the baths.

The church has an old wooden tub, just big enough to sit in with knees drawn fully up. A firebox in one end is stoked to heat the water, and a wooden partition divides the firebox from the main part of the tub. One washes thoroughly outside, shivering on a wooden platform above the cement floor, splashing warm water over one part after another, until clean. Then comes the step into paradise. Steeping in the hot water warms body and soul to the core. The tub at the church is not heated regularly, the same water is used by everyone in the household, and sometimes a green disinfectant is added. But it is the first physical relief from the winter cold, comfort that needs no translation.

Eventually the neighborhood bathhouse becomes part of a routine, though after a cold day even the anticipation of limitless hot water is barely enough to motivate my first step out the door. Into the winter night, bundled in hat, scarf, overcoat, boots. Pay a few yen at the door, take a small wooden locker, undress in the cold, then quickly slide the old wooden doors open and closed. Inside there are white tiles, a dozen or more spigots, little wooden stools to sit on, and all the hot water one could wish to splash anywhere. The back wall has a faded pastel mural of green mountain springs and an ocean beach. The central tub features hot water trickling in at one end, and space for eight or ten people to soak. The main problem is that most people already in the tub have found the places where the temperature is ideal. Newcomers must either get in close to the inflow and tolerate the higher temperatures, or get in at the other end where it can feel tepid, or wait for someone to leave. Soon I learn the routine, each visit helps to acclimate my skin to the hotter areas, and gives opportunities to watch what others do to regulate the tub to their liking.

On the walk back home from the public bath I am a different being. Warm to the core, hatless, coat and scarf open, clean and happy. The glow can last for hours, well past the trip upstairs to sleep between icy cotton sheets and heavy futon mats. From the window on the landing the volcanic profile of Mt. Iwate appears, standing watch over the snowy city. Its right-hand slope is reminiscent of Fuji.

Northern winters do thaw and eventually break up into cold springs. Moments of promise, then icy relapses. The process is frustratingly slow, much like the way that cultural adjustment develops. Daylight broadens long before the real warmth arrives, and breakthroughs come at unexpected times. In the same way, understanding of the surrounding culture deepens long before one is really able to act on it. One becomes dependent on new friends for contact and invitations, but friends have their own lives and are not always on hand. Gradually self-reliance arrives. Knowing the name of a thing gives one power over that thing: *onion, bus stop, laundry,* then *discount, small change, flounder,* and eventually *collect call, reservation, thank you I have had enough.* Food, haircuts, introductions, banks, trains, and finally even the telephone become routine.

After three or four months in the loft above the church, I get my own place to stay. There are two rooms, a small kitchen, and even a blue plastic Japanese bath, at the end of a bus line well out in the country. Surrounded on all four sides by rice fields, it is still only a couple of kilometers from the school. With considerable help from fellow teachers I accumulate bedding, a television, and kitchen belongings and begin to live on my own for the first time in my life. Soon the place is home. Best of all, the girl back home applies for, and gets, a teaching job in the same city. Trusting to luck, she flies halfway around the world and I am there to meet her. Initially she rooms with a doctor's family in town.

III

It was a great idea to bring a banjo to Japan. Guitars may be played around the world, but the voice of a five-string banjo with its high drone string sparkles in a way that clearly says "America." Every few weeks I ask permission to take the banjo into my English classes. We do easy American songs, silly ones like "There's a Hole in the Bucket," a field holler "Another Man Done Gone," beautiful ones like "Shenandoah." I usually have to translate the words one by one. For the students it is a break from the strict lessons of the national curriculum. But more than that, these classes are just plain fun.

In my second year of teaching, I talk to the seniors about Tom Sawyer and Huckleberry Finn. About the challenge of being young and setting out on your own voyage of discovery. This clearly has a lot of appeal, and also serves as a sort of explanation of why I am there among them as well. It is not part of the main curriculum.

Life as a teacher involves meetings. The Principal speaks first, then the assistant, then the senior teachers. The detached, polite rhetoric can take hours. The leaders do not necessarily make the decisions but they do speak first, last, and often. Those lower in the order who have something to say must wait, often for long periods. Eventually I learn that my opinion can also be voiced here and by trial and error I learn to speak too, within the social protocol of the faculty.

One day an emergency meeting is called for the entire faculty. A senior has been discovered eating a meal and drinking liquor at a local restaurant during school hours. The punishment should be expulsion from school but graduation is only a few weeks off.

The main concern at first is not the boy and his future but rather the loss of face that the school has suffered. Nearly everyone who speaks apologizes for shaming the institution by not having given enough guidance to the scapegrace, Kenjiro. I have had him in my classes, and he is almost the only student who has ever been openly rude to me.

Despite imperfect grammar, poor use of honorific expressions, and occasionally speaking out of turn, I do take part in this meeting and others like it. I weigh in with the teachers who favor allowing Kenjiro to graduate. Eventually he is not expelled but allowed to receive private instruction and testing at home. The meeting lasts until well after dark. An American newcomer to patience and protocol, I am learning to be a part of decision-making in a foreign language. It is a valuable lesson that will be useful for years to come.

Good feelings grow, pride in who I am and what I am doing, a love of the local food and local expressions, and despite my foreignness an increasing sense of equality with my co-workers, a real source of joy. Most importantly, awareness dawns of what is really at the rock-bottom of a sense of well-being. I need work and a peer group, a space of my own, a few familiar foods, warmth…and exercise.

After school there are sports and culture club activities. I often practice with the school's basketball club, and very much enjoy the chance to be competent at something. But whatever else is happening in life, I find I need to cover ground with my own two feet, until I get tired, and to do this on a regular basis.

The principal, a runner in his youth, schedules an all-school cross-country run once a year. The runners do not just mass at the starting line, however. An opening ceremony is held, and students line up by home room. Everyone, even many of the teachers, runs five or six kilometers under the bright October sky, and receives an apple. Then there are a closing ceremony and awards. No match for the faster kids, I settle for finishing something like 60th place and the apple tastes delicious.

The freedom of living alone lets me rediscover running in my spare time. There are country roads to stride along, and my own supply of hot water for bathing at home afterwards. I run regularly up and down the long banks of the Kitakami River, or across the fields and down rural roads to the little country train station. Spring brings water, frogs speaking in single haiku or in massive oratorios. After the rain comes the wilting heat of summer, and I must run early or not at all. In the beautiful Japanese autumn, rice sheaves hang on long poles and children fly kites in the fields before faint mountains outlined in the haze from distant straw fires. Even the long cold winters offer discoveries, such as snow caps on the stone fox-god at the *Inari* shrine. Running makes me feel invisible, and exclusively myself. Seldom do I ever see others out on training runs except at the school grounds, though I know members of school track clubs and at least one physical education teacher at my school who run regularly. Despite being a *gaijin*, nearly six feet tall and only twenty-five years after the end of the war, I feel that I am seldom noticed when I stride past a rural intersection and out alongside the rice fields beyond. Perhaps I am just too strange a sight to register with the local observers. Or perhaps I am too caught up in my own momentum at that moment to care, and that too is part of why I need to run.

Running helps me focus on what I need to do at work as well. Gradually I get accustomed to the rules of life and in the process Japanese society starts to feel like a normal, sensible format for life. Exercise helps maintain the balance. School takes five and a half days a week, so it is only Saturday afternoon and Sunday that I have time to run much on my own. But those long afternoon runs in the humid cold or the humid heat, in heavy canvas basketball shoes (the only size tens I can find), ending in a warm soak in my blue plastic Japanese bath, come to be an essential part of my two years of teaching, two years that shape the rest of my life.

IV

The English teachers have gone out for a few drinks, and afterwards one or two that know me best invite me along for another drink before going home. We stroll through the snowy streets of Hachiman-cho, the traditional entertainment district near the main Shinto shrine. Ducking into one very small bar, we find dim light, seven or eight stools, and a couple of patrons. A few minutes later, one of the patrons turns toward us, bearlike, grunting drunkenly in a thick local brogue. He is telling me something from the heart, and it is not pleasant. This was not in my first-year language course. My colleagues tell me not to worry, but they appear worried. The man pulls his shirt open and grasps a loose fold of belly skin and fairly roars about it. There is a scar there. One of my friends tells me in English that the man was in the war and was wounded by American troop fire. The man is claiming that the Germans had the right answer, that Americans are scoundrels. There is an expectant pause, an opening for me to say something. First, I am sorry that he was hit by any bullet, particularly one from my country and I try to tell him so. This is not fully understood. He repeats his assertion that the Germans as a people have the right approach. All I can think of is that many Americans such as Eisenhower have German ancestry. This stops his tirade but it clearly won't change his mind. The three of us finish our drinks and once outside my colleagues apologize profusely. I have not been offended and try to say so. I have heard bigotry and war tales used to justify each other in my own country, in more stories, comics, and jokes than I can count. It is almost refreshing to hear it from the other side.

In eight years of living in Japan, no other experience like this takes place. Yet every time I return to the U.S., I hear pejorative remarks about Japan, celebrations of the flight of the *Enola Gay* and the bombing of Hiroshima. Perhaps Americans hold onto our wartime stereotypes longer because we were victors. Or is it just because we are Americans and preoccupied with ourselves? Why have so few of us learned anything about Japan since the war ended?

Several of my teaching colleagues share their wartime experiences too. Some were born in Manchuria. Many tell of severely restricted diets. One was in the Navy near Alaska working as a code expert monitoring U.S. transmissions, and went on to become an English teacher. Another trained as a teenage pilot in a suicide squadron, discovered the beauty of the earth from aloft and went on to teach geography.

V

"Are you going to have a Japanese wedding?" It is an innocent-enough question. Somehow, it feels artificial though. My wife-to-be feels the same way. We are two *gaijin* in a very traditional society and both have many Japanese co-workers and friends. But neither of us is Japanese. Nor are we marrying into a Japanese family. We will live in a Japanese house, because that is appropriate to what we are doing and part of our experience.

Even though we are children of the sixties, and designing one's own weddings is all the vogue, we would certainly feel uncomfortable dressed in a wedding kimono, *tsuno-kakushi* headdress and formal *hakama* before people who understand the meaning of those garments far better than we do.

After some reflection, we do design our own ceremony and invite many Japanese friends including the principals of the respective high schools where we teach. But our clothes, the ceremony and the person we choose to preside are Western in origin, and we find this is what means the most to us. Later, our Japanese friends throw a reception for us in their style, which makes everyone feel better. All traditions have been observed.

VI

I am sitting in the pre-dawn dark, facing a paper screen and trying to fathom the stillness.

There is no motion but only mind, mindful of the thoughts parading like willow leaves afloat on the stream, mummers' floats glaring in parade, bicycles trains strollers delivery trucks passing always passing, and yet trying to empty my mindful mind of all thought.

Trying not to knit brows in the effort to press my spinal column away from its natural curve and hold it in a straight line, the shortest distance between brain and...the cushion on which my coccyx rests grounded, mindless of the vestigial legs that cross and ache, protest and beg for exercise. So little is going on, so much is flooding the mind. The eye sees only a spot on the screen, level with my position. There is so much to notice.

An acolyte ran through the halls moments ago ringing a bell loudly to summon all sleepers, deny the mind the completion of a satisfied night. One by one we rolled our mats and silently shuffled to the meditation hall.

This is *Zen* meditation, of the Soto variety in which there are no verbal puzzles, no unsolvable conundrums, only physical straightness and stillness. A straight back is a straight mind. Every activity has a prescribed order, so that life may focus on the greater presence of truth rather than the smaller presence of satisfaction.

I am aware that the *roshi* is passing behind me. A sudden tap on my shoulder. As I have been taught, I bow towards the wall and wait. The wooden lath stick whaps the back of my shoulder blade and stings. I bow again. The dark-robed figure behind me silently glides away down the line of meditating silhouettes, both Japanese and Western. Suddenly I am aware that the spot on the screen level with me now is six inches higher than the spot I had been looking at.

After ninety minutes, the session is over and the group breaks our fast, again silently except for the crunch of a *takuan* pickle that a novice has not yet learned to muffle with a bite of rice.

The following Monday, I am supposed to teach English conversation but find this nearly as great a challenge as the meditation exercise. My mind is now so mindful of the silent events that occur there constantly that I can hardly focus on what to say to another person. I could converse with a pillar more easily than with a student. The weekend Zen retreat passes, but the lessons in some way remain.

There are monks on Mount Hiei whose meditation exercise consists of running, running all through the night, in any weather, running until the mind itself is empty of any awareness. Perhaps I have been running the whole time I have been in Japan, perhaps I run only when I run. But in some way I sense a kinship with the monks of Hiei. In daily life, running is both my means of excluding awareness and enhancing awareness, and I now know that this is no contradiction.

VII

The end of the assignment arrives. After years of being treated as a guest, I am able to speak and to understand, stay afloat and in some ways even thrive. My dreams are sometimes in Japanese, my gestures no longer entirely American. Still a goldfish, still conspicuous, I am nevertheless at home in the deep waters of another culture.

A bowl of hot noodles on a train platform in the early morning, rice cakes warmed on a wood stove in winter, frogs singing in the rice fields under a spring moon are now familiar and dear. At the same time, it is hard to find clothes, shoes, eyeglasses, and there are still cultural obstacles like knee pains from sitting and the way the annual "forget-the-year" party at work always seems to fall on December twenty-fifth, when carousing just doesn't feel appropriate.

Does one continue to swim out of sight of land and become a creature of the "other" culture? Born and raised in the comfort of one world, why commit to another where we will never be native? I will never grow fins and gills, but my offspring, if raised in the host culture, will.

My wife and I take a long, low-budget trip around Southeast Asia, with rural bus rides in Laos, hiking in the hill country of northern Thailand, a freighter passage to Borneo, and time to go into upriver Sarawak and a Balinese home. Afterwards, back in

Japan and treading deep water in the host culture again, I make a decision. Not to swim so far out from shore that I lose sight of who I am. For my wife, the experience ignites an interest in anthropology, and becomes her career. And then there is a long flight back to the United States.

For the record, the health of the Reverend, my first host, declined under the effects of his heavy drinking in the years after I moved out on my own. The young woman who had been our domestic helper, however, learned to be a typist on the traditional one-handed Japanese typewriter. The last time I saw her she was well-dressed and attractively made up. She told me she was earning a good paycheck, and flashed a smile that glowed with confidence. The good works of the Reverend are clearly living after him.

Years later, I run into one of my students. He eagerly tells me that after I left and he had graduated, he and another student spent much of the summer building a raft from scavenged materials. They talked about Huckleberry Finn and the Mississippi and remembered the classes they had with me. Eventually they launched the raft on the Kitakami River and found that it was difficult to steer and that the river had shallows that were hard to avoid. He tells me, sheepishly, that they only got as far as Ishidoriya, perhaps fifteen miles down the river. I grin right along with him, though, because clearly building a real raft meant a lot to him and he is genuinely happy to have found me to tell about it. I may be the only person in his life who really understands why he built that raft.

PART TWO, 1979–1984
Tokyo

VIII

Five years have passed. We have two children. I have degrees in Far Eastern languages and business, and have now returned to Japan to work in a Japanese company doing accounting. The river continues to flow, as the ancient writer Chomei said, but the water itself is never the same.

Accounting work fills each day and many nights. The parent company provides a good salary. I am not a manager but a line worker, precisely because my language skills allow me to be one of the multitude. At first, newness and curiosity are natural. Then immersion in our common workload quickly forces the group back to coping with numbers. In no time I am one of a team and pulling my share of the team's weight.

Having taught in the Japanese public school system, I am far ahead of other foreign businessmen in understanding my co-workers' backgrounds. I still eat bread or rice both literally and symbolically, and try to back up this statement in the way I work.

Stacks of news and announcements in Japanese are circulated from desk to desk under the soft fluorescent glare, for me to read, initial, and pass on. The office din of telephones and low conversation is permanent. Change is rare. Meetings follow the same protocols that I learned nine years previously, the same emphasis on agreement. To disagree is to invite extended discussion from all sides until a new consensus response can be identified and agreed upon. One section meeting goes overtime when a new arrangement of desks is discussed. The secretary does not feel comfortable because one set of file drawers will be facing in a direction opposite all the others. The arrangement makes no difference to me, but she is a group member and has raised the issue in a formal meeting. The others think I should have an opinion. Her concern is treated seriously and discussed for nearly an hour before she joins in the agreement and the arrangement is accepted.

Each year, there is a ceremony on the anniversary of the company's founding. On this occasion the President, who normally speaks first at all ceremonies, defers in favor of a diminutive woman from the payroll section. She joined the precursor of this company during the war era, and has a year more seniority than he has. Normally extremely quiet, she rises to this occasion in a new way every year, regaling the assembly with stories such as how she saved a week's wages, three yen, to see a movie in Hibiya during the war years. This departure from normal protocol is in fact an extreme exception that proves the rule of hierarchy, and at the same time a strict observance of another special rule, that of respect for seniority.

"Excuse me for going home before you do." The suits may all be gray-blue, the only female a secretary, and green tea constantly in the cups, but we accountants consider ourselves socially progressive. Out company does not work Saturdays. Also, during peak work periods only those with the bulk of the work on any given day work late. It is acceptable to apologize and go home early, say at 7:00 p.m., even though someone else will be working until midnight. In a few days, the logjam of work tasks will shift and those who left early will have to stay late.

One cannot work closely with others and not get to know them as individuals. Unlike the U.S., however, one does not speak of one's own accomplishments in making small talk. It is said that the nail that sticks up gets hammered down. As occasions demand, there are evening parties at which everyone's attendance is assumed, jokes and stories told, friendships formed. I learn that a colleague once placed sixth in the all-Japan singles tennis tournament. Another is raising his children in the same house where he grew up, sending them to the same school he attended, where they are taught by some of the same teachers, a relative rarity in cosmopolitan Tokyo.

IX

Bread-or-rice questions exist for Japanese people, too. Perhaps that is why they ask me the question so often. One night as we work late, the oldest member of the group has a suggestion. "Let's try McDonalds," he tells the secretary who is going for take-out food. "I haven't had bread for dinner in a long time." This is not for my sake, because I have told him I hardly ever eat at the Golden Arches. He is just looking for variety. I chuckle, and try to explain that to me a hamburger means eating beef, that we speak of eating chicken, beef or fish, Chinese or Italian. But in vain. To him, a hamburger is bread for dinner.

A highly skilled, bilingual executive secretary confides in me. She is losing patience with both the Japanese and American directors she works for, and needs to vent.

"They (the Japanese directors) just write numbers on a paper, or rearrange the words, but written very very plainly, for us to retype, so we don't have to think about what we are doing. They don't have us think, or give us any room to decide how to do the work they've given us.

"Tell me, don't American managers sometimes expect their secretaries to write a letter for them, I mean to know how to take a message and make a suitable letter out of it? Don't they expect a secretary to correct a word if it's misspelled? Here in Japan, a Japanese man gets upset if you change anything. He wants everything just the way he wrote it, and sometimes they really get it down wrong, you know, but they want it written out just like that."

But there is another side to the coin. Her tone gets more emphatic.

"We are polite to you foreigners and that's *because we are Japanese*. We know how to serve tea, to smile and laugh at your jokes, and we will do whatever work you give us. We treat you *as a guest*. But our own people don't like to see us seriously taking dictation, because they don't know what it is. Do you know, the other day Director Yamada saw me sitting in front of Director Murphy's desk taking dictation (she imitates a pose of a stenographer concentrating on a tablet) and afterwards he scolded me! He *scolded* me, said I shouldn't sit there like that! 'Why do you just sit there with your head down, it looks terrible. Don't you know that you should keep an open attitude, keep your spirits up, and don't ever let your boss's anger get you like that, don't ever show that you feel bad.' He thought Director Murphy was scolding *me*! He'll never understand why you have to look at a tablet if you're writing shorthand on it, that that is something that can really help, and we can write letters, that we're not just ornaments.

"But otherwise, you foreigners, if you don't want to learn how we Japanese are, we really don't care whether you're here or not. We are Japanese, so we will treat you *as guests*, and smile and be nice and make *coffee*, but we really would just as soon you went back to Houston. Go ahead, go back to your Houston, and you won't be able to complain about the way *we* do things here. We'll send you your salary and bonus money, just like now (she gestures mailing an envelope) and you can just be happy there. As long as you're here, we will treat...you...just as *A GUEST*!"

I am laughing before she finishes, and then we both laugh together. It is all too true. Exceptionally skilled as a secretary, she is unhappy both ways. Her American bosses treat her as a competent stenographer and editor, something her Japanese bosses feel is not only outside her job description but even demeaning. Yet she reserves her most scathing criticism for the American managers who come for two- or three-year overseas stints, accept the Japanese smile and hospitality, and then leave for higher-paid positions somewhere else in the world. The word *guest* is progressively more loaded with each repetition.

X

The seasons come and go. Summer in Tokyo is oppressively hot and muggy, autumn clear and exhilarating, winter dry and windy, and then comes spring. The other accountants joke that they never see cherry blossoms by daylight because the annual year-end account closing cycle involves heavy overtime work from early March through late April. At home we eat more rice than bread, but I also discover a Japanese baker who sells wonderful whole-grain bread he learned to make while traveling in Denmark. My own children start school. Japan is home again.

XI

"When are you going back to your country?" The question is always asked eventually. Some foreigners do adopt Japan as a permanent home, and as we get more fluent in speaking the language and functioning in society, we find that it would in fact be possible to stay. Visas and work could be arranged, long-term housing procured, schooling for children figured out, and thousands of foreigners do in fact do this. Yet our Japanese friends keep asking us when we are leaving. We know you came from somewhere, and sooner or later you are going back. Aren't you? You are not going to stay here with us, not going to be part of our lives forever.

It is the same question as the earlier one about having a Japanese wedding. I am often mistaken for Japanese over the telephone, bow reflexively when thanking or parting from others, read the morning paper and drink cup after cup of green tea at work. I have grown out of the nervous habit foreigners have of raising the pitch of their voice in Japanese, and have learned to speak more in my own natural timbre. Yet the question does not seem to have an answer, or perhaps I have been focusing on learning and would like to be recognized for what I have accomplished, not for the uncomfortable fact that I never will be Japanese and can only approximate being a member of this society.

The company takes over my life far more thoroughly than a job "back home" would. The high school where I taught years earlier would have done this too, except that I lacked the language and social skills to carry the work that other teachers bore. Now, as a regular corporate salaried employee I have a full set of duties requiring me to read, speak and write in Japanese and observe all the social conventions of the workplace. From green tea to staying late. I am discovering that with a good bit of effort I am able to do this, and the discovery is reassuring. The work is often exhausting, but my co-workers are just as tired.

Working late one evening on a thorny deferred tax accounting problem, three of us are given free coupons for taxi rides home by our section manager as a reward. By ten o'clock the problem is resolved and we head for the elevator. The same thought occurs to each of us, and by the time we are out of the building on the night streets we head around the corner for a beer or two before going home. My two co-workers are pretty good at English but seldom use it at work, and by eleven we are all chuckling about our "deferred taxi," knowing that we have violated company policy by accepting the prepaid taxi rides and not using them to go straight home to rest and family as our boss intended.

An older co-worker talks to me of a problem he wrote about in his college years. A child, born into the world, cries because its birth is painful yet adults and children rejoice and feel warm about the arrival of another person. At death, a person often feels calm, contented and relieved of a burden but relatives, children and friends weep and are pained. What is it, then, that brings us pain and joy, anguish and release? Like a Zen *koan* or puzzle, this one won't admit of a rational solution. The best approach is to coexist with it. When knowledge does come it is almost certain to be in a form that words cannot frame, but that a nod, a gesture, will convey to another who understands.

I am aware that I am not Japanese and never will be. Japan in the 1980s has no experience with assimilating foreign immigrants. Even Japanese returning from overseas, where they have learned other ways, have difficulty fitting back in and often must send their children to private or international schools in their home country. Nails get hammered into shape, as the saying goes. Or they are forced to the side. Inwardly I have always known that I am in Japan on a journey, not to stay. This makes it increasingly difficult to straddle the gap between life in an Accounting De-partment where everyone around me will stay until their working days are done, and private musings about what other journeys might lie ahead in my life.

We have already begun to stretch towards the next event in life. Each weekend I take the sleeper train northward to Morioka to spend Saturday and Sunday with my wife and our two young children. She is conducting interviews there for her doctoral research. This arrangement gives me escape from Tokyo but also plenty of weekday evenings and mornings alone to contemplate the implied permanence of life in an office.

Escape, again, comes in the form of running. I have purposely chosen a house close to the bank of the Tama River. Living by a river was no luxury years ago in the cold north, but is a real blessing in Tokyo where elbow room is so severely restricted. Monday through Thursday nights I come home from work, and run. As the summer approaches, I can also run early mornings before work. The miles pile up. The mental release, the pulse of movement are wonderful. The river bank is open space for everyone, with hundreds of people flying kites, walking dogs, riding dirt bikes, or playing baseball. But seldom do I see other runners, just as I seldom saw runners when I lived in the North. This seems strange because Japan has a proud tradition of distance running.

Thousands of Japanese runners participate in traditional long-distance team relays called *ekiden*, a tradition that goes back to the days when messages were relayed by runners along the main roads. Seven different Japanese runners have won the Boston Marathon. Toshihiko Seko is a celebrity at the top level of world distance running in the 1980s. Yet the river bank on a beautiful weekday evening seems virtually devoid of anyone doing what I am doing. Where do all these runners train? I run up one side of the river, cross a bridge, run back downstream and cross another, then return home. Eventually I go an additional bridge or two in either direction, making a loop nearly ten miles long. The runs get longer.

One weekday morning I am striding along the Kawasaki side of the river when a boy of perhaps eleven comes up and runs alongside me, at first without effort but wordlessly. After a mile at about an eight-minute pace it is getting difficult for him to keep up, and we are approaching the Maruko Bridge where I will cross back over to Tokyo. As we stride up onto the bridge, he asks "How far are you going?" I tell him truthfully that I've been running for two hours to that point, and am going to run the Kawaguchi International Marathon. His eyes get big. I am clearly international, a runner, and going a long way. At the far end of the bridge he turns back to recross to Kawasaki. I can see he is going to have a story to tell.

Somewhere, a decision is made. Running has always been an escape from something. I am suddenly aware that it is now an escape *to* something as well.

XII

Two-thirty in the cold of a November night. The six-year-old, the four-year-old are sound asleep. My wife barely stirs. Downstairs on tiptoe, coffee, juice, piece of toast and nothing more. Ahead of schedule, yet too excited to stand around. Back the car out of the small driveway. Forward, a right and a left through tight neighborhood lanes. And out onto Kampachi Road. The broad avenue is deserted except for street lights, traffic lights, here and there a storefront light. Flying over and through one intersection after another, my white Corolla pulls onto the Chuo Expressway and minutes later whizzes through the outer Tokyo suburbs, then climbs into low hills. Exit signs and kilometers tick by at speeds seldom experienced by daylight.

The only companions now are dark sky, the brilliance of my own headlights against the green expressway signs and the dazzle of roadside reflectors. The first steps out the door are already behind me, the journey under way. The early moments are always painless, exhilarating. Training runs of seventeen to twenty miles have taught me the habit of not spending mental energy too early though, and the long-distance runner's routine of checking and re-checking is already well established. The gear is in my bag, the race number, shirt, jacket, shoes, socks, clothes for afterward. Heartbeat normal, muscles will be normal after a stretch. Fluids, band-aids, check. What about sense of humor.

I brought it, but it's in the bottom of my bag somewhere. This event is between me and myself and I will be very interested to see how it turns out. Nobody at work knows about it, and only a handful of friends have been told. Nothing lost if it doesn't work. Success, such as may occur, will be also primarily for my own appreciation.

In the town of Kawaguchi-ko the streets are unfamiliar in the starlit blackness but downhill leads to the lake. The row of lakefront hot-spring hotel-bathhouses is ahead. Parking on the street is easy to find in the middle of the night. Already in my running gear, I doze in the car, now and then turning on the engine for a little more warmth.

Already there are dark shapes striding through the streets, more than two hours before the start. Who could possibly be loosening up at this hour? Only a runner intent on the experience of running, someone supremely confident of being able to last the full marathon distance, already focused on the act of preparation.

I am focused too, but have resolved not to burn up much energy in pre-race activity. There will be miles enough out on the course once the gun goes off. If it takes me the first thirty minutes of the race to warm up, then that's half an hour of race time and perhaps six kilometers well spent. To me, there is comfort in knowing that this will help shorten the race. Those shapes sprinting intently through the dark must be relying on self-knowledge gained in some other way.

Stars begin to dim and in the predawn light the white mass of Mt. Fuji looms beyond the dark waters of the lake. More cars are arriving, runners in warmup gear, swathed in hats and scarves against the cold, making their way down towards the lakefront. My inner checklist has by now repeated itself many times and is starting to feel stale. I take a last gulp of water, kick the car door open, stand up and fill my lungs with icy mountain air.

Patches of ice reflect up from the gutters. The night is just below freezing. Moment by moment the morning light is grow-

RUNNING THE SEVEN CONTINENTS

ing, constantly altering the shades of red, gold and white cast on the great mountain.

Here and there, groups of runners are stretching in unison, some doing the morning radio calisthenics routine that I learned twelve years ago as a schoolteacher. Identical warmup suits suggest that these are running clubs. Other runners stretch alone, staring out onto the lake or up at Fuji. White breath puffs hang in front of each face before vanishing in the dry mountain air. It is too cold to stand still for long.

Eventually there is a crowd forming at the starting line, and we are encouraged to line up by predicted time of finish. Now we are standing close enough that speaking to strangers is natural. Some are from nearby cities, Shizuoka, Chofu, others from far enough away to have spent the night. Many around me have run marathons before. This is my first time though I only volunteer this if asked directly. The advice is the same – *gambare* (persevere, hang in there) – that is offered for work, studying or any other effort.

This is only the fourth race of my life. The others were just community runs with only a few hundred entrants. Now the crowd of starters is well into the thousands, and the sanitary facilities at the start are overwhelmed. Runners are taking advantage of any bush or tree at the start. In well-mannered Japan this seems laughable, and I am actually elated to see necessity and common sense overtaking social norms for once.

The speaker at the front is too far away to hear well, and there is too much chatter in the pack of runners. When to start my watch is not clear. Suddenly I see runners moving at the front of the start area and it is time to punch the start button. Then, with a hop, a shuffle, a step, a longer step, and at last a stride, it begins.

Now there is no turning back. In fact, there was no turning back when my alarm went off hours ago in the dark back in Tokyo. No, it was before that, the day I set out on my twenty-mile training run and shuffled home in city traffic too long after sunset. Or was the first step the day I set up a training journal to log miles and plan longer runs? Or was it the day I saw the announcement of this race in the magazine? Somewhere running changed, from being pure escape to being a step towards this run. This marathon.

The thousands of runners string out as we turn onto a bridge, crossing over an arm of the lake in a short "parade" loop back into the town for the first five kilometers. The slap of running shoes on pavement is a continuous background to the chatter in the crowd. Some twenty minutes later we are passing the start again, legs beginning to loosen, and this time heading out of town for two loops around the lake shore. The sun is beginning to touch the autumn colors on the nearby mountains, the sky turning a pale early-morning blue.

Soon my children will be stirring at home. Eating last night's rice, or this morning's bread, or both. Their favorite shows and books are in Japanese, their chatter mostly in English. We have chosen international school. Some of our Japanese friends have reacted to this with dismay but Japan's schools are hard places for any child who looks or acts different.

I have the skills to work here, have put in the time to understand and love much about Japan. I have come here twice and stayed four years each time. As I look up at the bright autumn of Kawaguchi, I know that I will not choose to live out my days here, however.

No Zen master would waste time looking for the moment that my goals changed, or even looking for the goals themselves. The proper way, this cold morning in the mountains, is simply to act. *Ha!* The marathon is not in front of me, it is one and the same with me. I am the marathon. So is the young guy beside me with a white cloth tied around his head. And the petite woman in the green warmups solemnly striding along in front of him. We are not only working on a problem; it is working on us.

Who are these people, where do they train, why are they running? Marathon running is not a requirement in this or any other country. There is no protocol that says the Principal or the President must run first, no requirement to stay next to your neighbors so that neither finishes before the other. Some arrived and warmed up in groups, but even as members of a running club they are making a personal choice to take on an activity that meets their own needs.

I have not told anyone at work that I am running this race. The time for that will be later. I will have no need to boast of it, assuming I do finish. Nor will many of those runners around me. One's deepest joys are to be downplayed. Each of us is here because of his or her own needs, striding along this lakeside road for a need that is purely personal. I am keeping my head up, my pace even and easy. A straight back is a straight mind.

Movement is effortless, breathing almost normal. We enter a tunnel in the hillside and a stiff headwind from the other side forces heads up and shoulders back until the far end is reached.

There is a glimpse of the race leaders where the lakeside curves into view. Soon they are too far away to see clearly, and in this two-lap race we will never see them again. In short order, the far end of the lake is reached and the road turns back into the gentle light of the rising sun. This is time to look back at those who are behind us, a chain of running humanity stretching back as far as we can see along the road we have already traveled.

Japanese like to say that they are one people, using expressions such as "we Japanese," or "in Japan, we do this," True, the same color of hair and eyes is a unifying factor as are centuries of history. But there are remarkably different features and coloring among individuals, and private opinions, if offered, can be remarkably diverse.

The Reverend, in his way, saw something in Russian religion that he felt was lacking in Japan and returned to do what he could to set it right. Kazuko struggled against a family and society that told her she would never amount to anything and almost succumbed to believing that. Teachers in my school struggled daily with the task of getting teenagers through the rigid requirements of the system. Some helped me struggle through too, either out of general courtesy on behalf of Japan or out of a hope that I would provide something for the students that the exam-driven school on its own never would. To truly eat rice I would have to struggle with the rigidity of exams, the inexorable expectations of university, job, marriage, children. And make my children do so too.

The rest of the first lap of the lake passes quickly. Passing the halfway point just before entering Kawaguchi-ko town again, we are among crowds of well-wishers clapping and shouting *gambare!* to particular runners or to everyone in general. Each of us is locked into an individual comfort zone, strides fixed, unwilling to speed up or slow down. There are water stations and the water is ice cold.

Before long we are on the second lap. The first one felt easier than on my trial run here several weeks ago. That is encouraging. How bad could the second one be? I have been keeping to my place in the string, but now and then I do pass a few runners. Perhaps I am actually well-trained for this thing. It doesn't matter how tired I get, because all I have to do is sleep afterwards anyway. Twenty-five kilometers passes. Not all of the road is familiar. Some bends I cannot remember passing before. We head back through the tunnel with its blast of cold air. Has it taken longer to get to the tunnel than it did on the first lap, or is that my imagination? Still I do not feel fatigued.

The thirty-kilometer mark approaches. I have been reluctant to alter my speed up to now, but we are well down the side of the lake and there are only a little more than ten kilometers to go. Gently, I begin to pass a few runners. Many around me seem to be slowing down rather than accelerating. A little effort moves me up perhaps fifty places, then another thirty, within no more than a mile. This is fun. I suppose once I reach the far end of the lake it will be time to pick up the speed again and see how far under 3:20 I can actually get.

The euphoria is brief. Very brief. Muscles that normally don't hurt until the morning after a long run are suddenly stiff and inflexible. Suddenly there is no comfort zone, no easy way to run at all. Each stiffness creates a new adjustment and more stiffness. I feel like stopping more than anything else, and before too long there is no choice. Walk but only for ten strides. Then for maybe twenty, then start to jog again. In less than a quarter mile, another walking break. This time the break is longer. Runners I passed only minutes ago are shuffling past me. I am hurting, panicking, and unprepared. Once I resume running I can catch them easily but the problem is that I can no longer run continuously.

So this is what hitting the wall is all about. Those other runners who slowed down around thirty kilometers were leaving the comfort zone too, but had the experience to do so gradually. Speeding up was the mistake of a novice. No, a fool. Perhaps this would have happened anyway, but we are not yet to the far end of the lake, and then it will be a long way back.

Any marathoner knows that fighting the wall is a matter of stop and go. Lurch and creak. Stiffly shuffling, sometimes walking, pushing back thoughts of "never again," I am still working this out as we reach the end of the lake and turn back to the east. Into the full light of the morning sun. The dazzle of the water on the waves, the bright reflection from the road surface, and the slap of the feet of runners are almost the only recollections I will have for the next half hour.

Eventually there are more and more runners in the same miserable state. It becomes apparent that some have trained better for the final miles than others. The rest of us suffer silently. One Japanese man perhaps ten years older than I is obviously fighting cramps in his legs. He lifts his gaze to Fuji, now ahead of us to our right. The eastern slopes are purest white in the full brilliance of the cold morning sun.

"Fuji, you are beautiful," he cheers. "My legs won't do a thing I tell them. But Fuji, you are beautiful!!" He is right. The mountain is standing beside us, a monument to purity, endurance, and Japan, and dozens within earshot silently agree.

Kilometers pass painfully, no longer one every five minutes

but more like seven, seemingly more. Do not ask for whom these distances are measured. We are all on a journey we undertook voluntarily, working on a problem that is now working on us with a vengeance. There is no argument, there is only the road, and the sharp slap of pain and alertness to the fact of the next step and the next. After a long time there are only three kilometers to go, then only two. The next kilometer feels like ten but suddenly there is only one and everyone freshens. Running again, in icy shade from buildings in town, then into sun around a turn onto a bright path into the parking lot where the race began…and about two hundred yards away a banner over the finish. Suddenly no pain can keep these legs from springing towards that banner. In the finish photo I am actually punching the stop button on my watch, conscious of a need to record the time for posterity. I have missed 3:20 by nearly fifteen minutes, all lost during the last ten kilometers of the race. But that was never really a goal. I have finished a marathon. And in doing this I have not only completed the escape I sought from the pressures of work and daily life, but discovered that thousands of Japanese have needed to do exactly the same thing. Instead of finding myself a loner in running, I have found that I am not alone at all. Runners around me are congratulating each other, and I join in and find I cannot stop smiling.

The lessons continue. The free soak in the hot springs that all finishers receive is not a good idea when one is already seriously dehydrated. A couple of chilled iced-coffee drinks and a cold cola, half an hour in a soft chair, and I am again able to stand and move slowly towards the car. There is more traffic on the Chuo on the drive home, yet for some reason I don't remember that trip at all.

The next Monday at work, I am walking stiffly, but go about the day with no undue ceremony. Many weeks later, an issue of *Joggers* magazine comes out. On the cover, Juma Ikagaa of Tanzania battles Toshihiko Seko and Alberto Salazar of the U.S. in the elite field of the Fukuoka Marathon. Inside, several articles deep, there are dozens of photos of the "people's marathon" race at Lake Kawaguchi, and I find that I am in one of them taken before the start. During a particularly slow part of the day, I quietly show the issue and the photo to two or three close co-workers. They tell a few others, and the picture circulates for ten minutes or so. That is enough. Any more would make me a nail that sticks out.

XIII

There one more annual section outing. This time I am allowed to be one of the major planners, and the others are interested to see what I will come up with. Breaking with tradition, I propose using public transport rather than a chartered bus, to save money, and spending the balance on a nice, very traditional Japanese *ryokan* in Izu that we normally would not be able to afford.

The outing goes wonderfully. The *ryokan* is a three-hundred-year-old wooden structure with a beautiful carp pond, wooden passageways, and improbably, a modern swimming pool tucked out of sight. The food is memorable. Songs and stories follow one upon the other well into the night. The secretary convulses everyone by doing imitations of each of us calling our wives to say we will be late coming home from work. She has my accent down amazingly well, and knows that I usually pick up bread, juice, and milk, and occasionally chicken, from the store at my local train stop. The eldest accountant in the group sees to it that everyone has an extra can of beer...for breakfast the next morning!

XIV

The taxi pulls over to where I stand at the curb. The driver flicks a lever inside, opening the rear passenger door for me. As we work back into the daytime traffic I ask him about his job.

They start early, as early as you can get there. I came in about 5:30 today and that's late. You can go as early as 4:00 if you want to.

The morning rush is short, and you're lucky if you get one good long-distance fare. Usually it's just men going from home to the nearest station, and that doesn't pay. Then you have to go back and look for another fare, because nobody wants a cab from a suburban station in the morning. So you use up time and gas by looking. You can just park and wait but that's not much good either.

Sure, we all have good days but you never know when it's going to happen. The best is if you get some company president after a party, and he's going to ride all the way back out to Yokohama or Saitama and doesn't care how much it costs him. But that hardly ever happens and most of them have their own drivers or get the expensive "hire cars" to take them. We regular taxis, we get the regular company workers and they mostly drink and then go home on the subway. It's not a good living.

I will drive as late as I can, after the last trains have stopped because that's when you can make money. We can go all the way to two o'clock if things are good and that's not often. It's a really long day. I drive every other day, three days one week and four days the next but Sundays aren't very good. On the days in between, all I do is sleep. Every other Sunday I get to do things with my kids.

Is it ironic that my last conversation on leaving Japan is as mundane and familiar as the first one? There has been so much else in between. We are all the products of the problems with which we grapple. The trick is to choose the right problems.

I pay the driver, add my sincere wishes for a safe day on the roads, and head for the city airport terminal. The years in the Japanese accounting office are up. I expected a transfer, but what was offered came as a complete surprise. The company is sending me to Australia, and in twenty-four hours I will be there. My family will come in a couple of months, and we will live in Sydney. But first I have a couple of jobs on the road. The first is to be in a city called Adelaide.

Book Bag

Among the more easily appreciated books of Japanese literature in the last century any list of my favorites would include the collection of Miyazawa Kenji's short stories, *Winds From Afar*.

Three works about World War II from the Japanese point of view that deserve a read are Ibuse Masuji's *Black Rain* about Hiroshima, and Ooka Shohei's *Fires on the Plain* and Michio Takeyama's *The Burmese Harp* about the war in Southeast Asia.

The incomparable *Tale of Genji* was written around AD 1000, may well be the world's first novel and certainly the first by a woman, and still ranks as one of the outstanding aesthetic texts in world literature.

Books on Zen and related aesthetics are as different and varied as the enlightenment experiences of the individuals who write them. The reader should try, experience and reflect, and perhaps understanding will come. Perhaps not. Or not yet. A runner, however, will understand the need to keep trying.

Australia

Hammond, South Australia, once a hard-working farming town, virtually uninhabited in 1984.

State Championship of Victoria Marathon Melbourne, August 1984

Central Melbourne

Yarra River

Finish

Start

M E L B O U R N E :

The route of the 1984 State Championship of Victoria
Marathon. The start and finish were along the Yarra
River in the center of the city, with most of the distance
along the bay front.

CHAPTER 3

One Fly Crawling Up a Window

Victoria State Championship Marathon, Melbourne, August 1984

> *Our fathers came of roving stock*
> *That could not fixed abide*
> *And we have followed field and flock*
> *Since e'er we learnt to ride;*
> *By river's camp and shearing shed,*
> *In land of heat and drought,*
> *We followed where our fortunes led,*
> *With fortune always on ahead,*
> *And always further out.*

A.B. "Banjo" Paterson, *The Old
Australian Ways*

I

A large, noisy group of runners is setting out on a run through the Adelaide greenbelt towards the surrounding hills. Expecting nothing more than a few miles on a Sunday morning, a newly arrived foreigner runs on the springy grass, moving alone in the opposite direction.

First one, then another local runner hails the stranger. "Why not run with us, mate? We're training for the marathon."

"Yes it's my first time here. I don't have an accent, *you* have an accent."

"I'm doing nursing at the uni, he's doing maths. How old are your kids?"

By the halfway point in the club run, below a waterfall in a green canyon, I have already been invited to a group breakfast at a pub near the park. On the return leg towards the city, when runners normally would be conversing less, new friends are still being made.

The Sunday run ends back in the greenbelt parklands. Eucalyptus leaves crunch underfoot. White clouds fly overhead, parrots fly to trees. Here every runner takes off one shoe, identified by the club membership "card," a colored and numbered plastic flap looped onto the shoelace. A hundred or more shoes go into a huge pile. The club secretary then draws shoes and awards prizes from local merchants. As each one-shoed winner hops up to claim his or her prize (and shoe), the crowd cheers and hoots approval under the warm autumn skies of May.

This is the South Australian Road Runners Club (SARRC), in the middle of a 40-week organized progression towards the city's Festival Marathon in August. The membership of SARRC ranges from students to 60-year-olds and up, from unemployed mechanics to the Premier of South Australia, John Bannon, himself a 2:40 marathoner ("fastest head of state in the world" according to SARRC buzz). The club has its own travel arm, SARRC Travel. Next Saturday, on a three-day weekend, there is a club trip to a rural festival in Melrose where there will be games, footraces, good beer and good times.

II

I go down to the Briscoes Bus Terminal at 7:30 Saturday morning like I've been told, and not recognizing anyone, stand around among the strings of jeans-clad Australians taking off for the weekend.

One bus is announced, and a couple tears off towards it trailing six or so tote bags and a staring toddler. I ask the people next to me, who wear running gear. It wasn't our bus, no our leader isn't here yet. Suddenly a fortyish woman with close-cropped hair and a commanding presence comes amongst us and things happen quite by themselves it seems. Bruce, she says, is flat on his back with back pains and she is just as glad to be out of the house all weekend and he'll be fine. In less time than it takes to comprehend that, we are all seated and counted. The baggage is stowed in the coach (*not* a bus), and "Geoff" its captain (*not* driver) is wheeling us up King William Street. The balcony at the rear of Parliament House is built for watching cricket, says Geoff, though if we want to know a lot more, Briscoes has a City Sights tour.

The enormous glass windows of our Volvo coach are a good clue why this is a favorite way to travel. Geoff banters good-naturedly with us and is promised at the outset that if he isn't a runner we will make him one. The Trans-Australia Highway takes us north over extremely flat, unremarkable land on the edge of the Bay of St. Vincent. At a rest stop, those who know each other munch cookies in small groups and the rest of us eye each other and the straight, level highway in shy silence. Runners like to run in groups and we are a group of runners, but we are not yet running together.

On board again, past port cities with livestock pens and ore smelters, then abruptly into low hills. The road winds into green, rock-strewn hills dotted with the mottled white trunks of leafy, graceful eucalypts along a twisting dry streambed. The hills grow quickly higher and drier, the trees larger and at the same time more gnarled and spreading, the pastures dotted with sheep under the blue sky. We roll through the little town of Melrose where tomorrow's festival will be, and on to stop at the crossroads called Wilmington.

The Wilmington Hotel, the only building of substance more than one story tall, stands before our gaze in time-worn glory, its dignity in a recent coat of green paint not quite hiding the scars of years on the frontier of the marginal farming and grazing belt. A few houses, one general store, one bakery on the street outside. Inside, the front room is a bar and billiard room, the back room a dining room. There are also a "lounge" for drinks and food, a kitchen, and a carpeted stairway with an old curved banister leading upstairs. The rooms are frontier, very neat, very plain, very adequate. Dressers upwards of thirty years old, maybe seventy, bathroom facilities at the end of the hall. The publican's wife is ill and Saturday night is the big night when all the locals gather here, so could we find our own lunch at the baker next door...? Yes, we can. But being runners, we would rather train than eat, and about a third of the group immediately heads down to a side road we've seen leading to "Alligator Gorge." Both foreign to the land and new to the group, I at least know how to run and will meet more people that way, so I head off with them hoping the alligator in the gorge doesn't work weekends.

Running in a group of seven, we enter low rolling hills with huge ghostly gum trees casting large shadows on emerald pastures. Clear blue sky and a correspondingly glaring sun gradually add to the heat we generate. Lynn and Gary, Lee and Sue and I run as far as the top of the first serious hill, and as they stop about thirty minutes into the run to fix a shoe I go up the next hill alone. A station wagon that has seen better days is parked at the top, on a wide road shoulder with a sweeping view of distant hills that could be sixty or seventy miles away in the clear dry air. "One of your mates went on ahead of ya" offers the driver of the wagon, and I recall seeing a shirtless guy with a pony tail running off ahead of us at the start. I decide against going after him, and turn for the run back, now sweeping fast down hills, flying back through the gum groves and over the dry ford until, where the dirt road levels out, I realize it is farther back than I thought. I do not catch up with the others until just before we reach the Inn. Time to shower and retire to the large room shared by the five single males (bachelor luxury!) for a nap. I know the English F.A. Cup soccer final will be on live at 11:30 that night and want to be awake for that.

Two hours later, I awake and wander into the TV room to learn that two of the other single males, Chris and Charles, have been pounding on the door because they'd locked the only key in the room when they went running. I hadn't seen them or heard them knock. Ah well, that's one way to get to know people.

Suddenly on a whim of the "captain," our entire group is on the coach again and off on a side trip to a ghost town. Everyone is back aboard and we wind out of Wilmington across the flat plains to the north and east. The tape plays Australian songs, one for Christmas about Santa's sleigh being pulled by four white kangaroos, another about coach captains.

> *He'd like to be leading us with a cattle prod*
> *He'd get us all back on the coach with no more than a nod*
> *And come to think about it, he looks just a little bit like God*
> *...he's your lover, he's your brother, he's your fairy-bloody-*
>   *godmother...*
> *He's the greatest...our Coach Captain.*

And of course, "Waltzing Matilda."

The captain explains that we are going to a town called Hammond, which once had over six hundred people in it and a blacksmith shop that employed thirty-five. Now there are only two. It seems that a hundred or so years ago one of the colonial fathers, a surveyor, had warned against settling beyond a line roughly from Port Augusta northeast towards Broken Hill in New South Wales. The line, he said, is like a shower curtain, with the tillable soil on one side and desert on the other, and no matter how rainy it looks the rain only falls on one side of the curtain. In a few good years, people settled and ranched in the area beyond the curtain, though, and prospered as recently as forty years ago, through the first big drought of the century. The second one, though, lasted twenty-two years, after which there was nothing left of Hammond or the capital of the people who had lived there.

As he talks, we cross what I take to be the shower curtain. From the green of the southern Flinders the land turns to gray-green sagebrush, and beyond Hammond, to brick red. We walk through a little curio museum, look into old buildings and the old pub. An old wagon sits right in the middle of what was once the town, as if the horse had just been unhitched and led to the stable.

Back in Wilmington, Saturday night is arriving. Locals are in the billiard room and at the bar, broad country accents, jeans, beer. A half-dozen or so women scurry through the dining room serving our mob of hungry runners. No longer very shy, more eager to talk, still more eager to eat, we are finding it a good time to exchange background stories. I eat with Andrew, the pony-tailed guy who ran away ahead of all of us, his wife Melissa, and their daughter Rebecca, an 11-year-old slyly quiet in the company of adults but a violin student and choir member who is making animated dinosaur films in a current school project. Andrew, a complete vegetarian, and Melissa, an avoider of all milk, butterfat, and most oils, are rather inconvenienced by country pub fare, but Rebecca and I eat everything we can get. Her parents say she doesn't distinguish Australian and American accents due to TV programming; sure enough, she (alone of the whole group) doesn't think I speak with an accent, and thinks all TV shows are Australian.

That evening we watch TV. There is an American film of the Weavers' reunion concert, then a film, "Sunday Too Far Away." This is an award-winner about sheep shearers and a strike that really happened, shot on location in South Australia not far from where we are staying. Now and then some of the runners acknowledge particular hardships of the shearing life that permeate the film. It's all new to me and a great introduction to being in rural South Australia. Finally it is time for the F.A. Cup, which Everton wins from Watford, 2-0. An older runner is rasping in an accent I can't understand about the game and is clearly overjoyed. It turns out he is from Everton (Liverpool) and has dreamed of a win for years. He works night shifts at a plant in Adelaide and was up for 48 hours before the game, then took a nap and almost missed it. Later I learn he has a grown son somewhere, lives in a single room, and has run incredible distances. He also drinks beer in unbelievable volumes – tragically, I think.

The next day the action is at the Melrose cricket/football oval, the center for the day's festival. The Mountain Run is set for 11:00, and after some time at rope-weaving demonstrations, we are off, about forty in all, locals and Adelaide SARRC tourists and me. After about two kilometers through pastures, the dirt fire trail we have followed begins to bend upward, first to a grade, then a gravel chute, then a boulder crawl, a 45° scramble under and over tree roots, emerging into a rocky moonscape. Finally there is a short flat shoot to the top. Having heard the record was 45 minutes I am pretty pleased with my time in the high forties, but also frustrated at doing as much climbing as running. So after a slug of water, I run back down, billy-goating along the rocky trail, finally emerging among a flock of fifty or so sheep in the upper pasture. The sheep skedaddle left and right, and still running downhill I shoot between them off through the gums. When the downhill ends, so do my legs – they have turned to rubber, and I force the pace back to the festival grounds but am fully spent. The whole round trip has taken me an hour and twenty minutes. I was eighth or so to get to the top (which, it turns out, was all that counted), but I am the first to get back to the fair by at least fifteen minutes.

Slowly the others trickle back, nobody with much starch left in them. There is groaning about how it was harder than something else they run every year, called Torture Ridge. The winner had done 34 minutes, it is announced, but the coordination in timing between start and finish has been primitive, so it is hard to tell what the time actually was.

The runners make up teams to enter the Tug-of-War. I don't think I have ever won one of those things and today, after running the mountain, doesn't seem likely to be the first. We give it our all and immediately lose to teams of locals in work boots.

Others go into pitching straw sheaves over poles, ride a wagon with Clydesdale horses, race bicycles, watch a boomerang thrower, drink beer or cokes, eat meat pies, steaks on bread, doughnuts from the Lions Club. Sammy Seagull makes an appearance for the kids. Another Family Fun Run is organized, announced as 5 kilometers. From the fact that Lee from our group wins it in ten minutes, it is obviously much shorter. Lee is fast, but that kind of time would get him into the Kentucky Derby.

The evening draws near, and after awards to the King, Queen, Man and Maid of the Mountain, our authentic bush dinner is laid out. It seems that about eight local Melrose people have run virtually the entire fair, and I've never seen anything better organized. They are continually producing and selling food, snacks, drinks, tickets, and coordinating the games. Many of our city-dwelling SARRC group have seldom or never tasted damper, a flat bread made in a frying pan. It is good, yeasty bread, heavy and hearty. There is stew, billy-can tea and bread-and-butter pudding. A local woman tells me that you must put a gum leaf in the tea or it doesn't taste right, also that you put newspaper in the pan for damper and when the paper browns it is just hot enough. If the paper burns it is too hot. One of the Adelaide runners quips archly that is has to be the *local* paper, of course. But it is clear that I, twice a tourist, am not the only one learning country ways this day.

Some of the group with sore legs, fatigue or children go back after dinner. The rest of us go to the barn-dance and yarn-spinning. Straw is spread on the floor of the main tent and wet down, and a three-piece band plays jigs and sprightly things. There is a Virginia Reel, several other dances in large sets, and at the end there is a square dance of terrific speed and complexity. Initially runners dance with runners, locals with locals, but before long all are mixing it up in a spree of whoops and flying straw. A Malaysian Chinese woman from our group is dancing the Reel with the "Coach Captain." The mood of the trip peaks here – partners switch and go back. I am asked to dance the first three dances by older wives in our group. Some couples are locals just over high school age, whose glowing faces and light steps are vividly saying to each other just what generations of Americans must have said at Saturday night barn dances before the advent of TV and disco. I have been to evenings of square dancing before and had fun, but nothing like this. This is no reconstruction. We are in the Genuine Article, and it has never died in Melrose. Legs that died on the mountain spring into life and the band drives everyone towards exhaustion, dance after dance.

For breaks, there is yarn-spinning. The host, a well-oiled local of evidently well-known reputation, calls for volunteers. Everyone who comes up front with a tale wears the "yarn hat," a broad-brimmed bush hat. Most of the yarns are standards. "An Englishman, and American, and an Australian are in a lifeboat together with only food for one…" Others are better. Three friends from Adelaide, Wilmington, and Myall (notoriously poor marginal farm land) had wives expecting children. The first, from Adelaide, had an eleven-pound son, very healthy, smart, athletic, and they had a party at a classy restaurant with good South Australian wine to celebrate. The second, from Wilmington, had a six-pound daughter, somewhat sickly and his wife had a bit of a hard time recovering. The friends had a quiet dinner at a pub, with some beer, congratulations and good wishes, et cetera. The third, from Myall, had a scrawny, premature, three-pound child with dull reflexes, a weak cry, and his wife barely pulled through, but they were alive. The friends threw an all-out party at the Adelaide Hilton with champagne, steaks, and a band. At which an acquaintance asked "Why did you all go to this expense? I mean he's your mate and all, but look at that little baby, it's really so weak you'd never expect much of it." The two from Adelaide and Wilmington answered, "That's all right, mate. When you're from Myall you're just glad when you can get your seed back."

Another recites a long "Casey at the Bat" type poem about a cricket match. Most of the yarns are better not set down in writing. Around eleven o'clock we remaining runners leave for Wilmington, dead tired.

One item on the schedule from the start has been a six-thirty run on Monday morning, a holiday, and considerable joshing has gone on about it all day Sunday. But I do find myself awake at six-thirty, and after a quick change and a stretch discover there are five other hardy souls of similar mind. It is a silent, slow jog, out dirt roads for thirty minutes, past a campground where a few sleepy campers are making coffee. We are roundly laughed at by a pair of kookaburras, the familiar cry surprisingly loud at close range. Being the only runners up makes it difficult for most of the group to keep going. The impending sunrise colors the beautiful bush country on all sides, and we do manage to make it back in just over a full hour. At the hotel I am able to grab a camera just in time to catch the last three returning with the dawn behind them.

On the way back the coach stops for good woolen knits, pottery, and lunch at the farming and wine center of the Clare Valley. Then we are racing a storm all the way back to Adelaide, the coach flying along as we freely exchange running stories, comments about the mountain, vows to come next year, and it isn't until the coach rolls into the terminal at Adelaide that the rain hits thick and cold and the reality of work, or classes, or in some cases life without work, falls again upon each runner individually.

III

Australia was home for two wonderful years. After many good years of working in Japan, years of attention to conformity, speaking in turn, not sticking out. The Japanese national character is said to arise from early populations of people who had to cooperate in irrigation, planting and harvesting. The Australian national character, however, originates from early populations of people who knew how to think for themselves and depended on individual ingenuity for survival.

There is a famous Japanese Zen puzzle in which one must imagine the sound of one hand clapping, an impossible exercise that intentionally frustrates the mind's desire to identify two opposing sides. There is no answer, only repeated frustration, and no escape until the mind finds a radically new view of the problem.

Japanese Buddhist thought stresses that one achieves true happiness only by escape from worldly cravings, including the craving for analytic solutions, for another hand to clap. Australians, on the other hand, will admit to betting on anything, even two flies crawling up a window, and will loudly and colorfully crave a favorable outcome. It's hard for me to say whether Australians have more fun with the contest itself, talking about it, or betting on it. What matters is that you're game, that you're in the game, that you're willing to take a chance, put your money on one side and trust your skill and rely on your mates to pull you through.

Running in Australia always made me feel exuberant to be in the race, competing hard yet not against others, in the game and challenged to keep up with the super-fit athletes around me but with a sense that competition brought out the best in all of us. Perhaps I was one fly crawling up a window, alone in my Japanese understanding that one does not win or lose in the long run. It would not have made sense to bet on my performance because there was nobody specifically racing against me. Still, I normally picked the closest runner to me in the race and ran as hard as I knew how. Always, I finished far back in the pack with those assumed to be just running for fitness. But I have never run faster in my life, before or since those two years in Australia.

To be sure, there are Australians who have not the slightest interest in sport (I have even met a few), but nearly everyone it seems can be induced to tell sports stories because these things are a matter of national culture and history. If one doesn't have a favorite team, a great game, or an individual hero, then one from Australian history will do.

A recent example is Cathy Freeman, winner of the 400 meters in the Sydney Olympics. Under intense pressure from the Australian media and public, she led the race from start to finish. Cathy Freeman boasts aboriginal family origins and therefore carried the pride of her own people as well as all Australians to the gold medal stand in a shining moment for Australian sport.

Professional running, complete with wagering, is noted in historical records at least as early as the 1840s.[3] The contest usually involves a number of heats in which losers are eliminated, and winners' performances analyzed and handicapped for the next round. Sprinters are assigned starting positions according to handicap. This makes it possible for runners of differing ability to compete in the same race, and for a slower runner with a large enough handicap to defeat a faster runner. A race is more than a race, because with a comfortable lead, a runner can slow up to get a better handicap for the next heat, and who can blame him?

My introduction to running against a handicap time, Australian style, came six months later in the Sydney Corporate Cup.[4] In early 1985, after I had been at the company in Sydney only a few months, word got out of my running and I was recruited for the CC.

Between noon and one o'clock on the appointed day of the week, my running co-workers and I would jog down along the harbor, past the world-famous Sydney Opera House, and into the urban greenspace called The Domain. Although entered as a team from the same company, teams do not have to run together. In fact, CC runners start at one-minute intervals throughout the hour, and the clock runs continuously. All finish at the same

---

[3] Douglas Booth and Colin Tatz, *One-eyed: A View of Australian Sport.* Allen & Unwin, 2000, p. 32.

[4] Sydney Corporate Cup information is available at http://www.corporatecup.coolrunning.au

spot, and report their times on the honor system, to the nearest five seconds. This not only spreads out the pack of runners through a fairly crowded park but also makes it possible for any CC participant to have a late meeting at work and still make it to the starting line.

What really distinguishes the Corporate Cup as a concept, though, is its clever scoring system. Each runner has a handicap time, and team points are only earned by individually beating one's handicap. But the faster one runs, the faster one's handicap will be in the next series, until it gets very difficult for the veteran runner to earn many points at all. There is even a method in this Corporate Cup madness. You'll see what I mean. Here's how it worked for me.

The first race was February sixth, and as I had no handicap yet I was advised to jog the course, enjoy it, and set a time I could beat the rest of the season. I recorded 29:05.

At that time the CC was held every other week so I showed up again, ready to score some points, on February twentieth. My handicap was my 29:05 from two weeks earlier, and I duly ran 27:45. For March sixth, the handicap was lowered to 28:30, and I beat it by a minute. On March twentieth, the handicap was down to 28:15 and I must have been primed to compete. I finished in 26:55, which remains my best time ever for the CC. For the last races my handicap stayed at 27:40 and though I beat that target a few more times I never did so convincingly enough that the CC people lowered it again.

For that first CC series, though, I earned the company team a bundle of points and the captain was happy. Though a much better runner than I, he had lowered his handicap over the years to 22:40. He seldom beat this by very much and consequently could score very little himself. In this way, the CC formula is intentionally "rigged" to favor the introduction of new runners. That is exactly what the organizers like, and what team captains who care about winning must do. Each season thereafter the first order of business is to find new runners who can score points and make the whole team look good.

The Stawell Gift is perhaps the leading example of professional sprint competition in the world, at a distance of 120 meters less handicap. It has been held in all but two years since 1878 and is still contested annually.[6] But Australians have also been known to run long distances for money, particularly if a bet was on the line. The professional distance runner Bill Emmerton is known for his runs in the heat of Death Valley, including one in which he wagered unsuccessfully that he could run twice as far as the American tennis hustler Bobby Riggs.[7]

The long list of great Australian runners who have won world championships includes the dominant distance runner of the late 1950s and 1960s, Ron Clarke; the world marathon record holders Derek Clayton and Rob de Castella; the champion Steve Monighetti and many others. But these stars are just the tip of a very large pyramid of Australians involved in sport of all kinds, and every level has its local teams and events in season. And its local legends, some of whom can be almost larger than life.

A living Australian legend is a Victorian potato farmer named Cliff Young, who discovered competitive distance running late in life and entered the Sydney-to-Melbourne race in 1983. The distance is a phenomenal six hundred fifty miles, and despite being nearly sixty years old, Cliff Young won it thanks in part to a stubborn avoidance of the sleep breaks that more experienced runners took. As the race wore on, Cliff's lead in the race attracted national attention on the nightly newscasts. And his reputation as a true man of the people was solidified at the finish when he shared his prize money among the other top ten finishers, declaring them all his "mates" and adding that it wasn't fair for anyone else who had run that far to go home with less.

As luck would have it, I actually competed quite closely with the legendary Cliff Young in a marathon, though I would not

---

[6] Stawell Gift information is available at http://www.stawellgift.com
[7] Gail Campbell, *Marathon: The World of the Long-distance Athlete.* Sterling, 1977, pp. 27–30.

become aware of the fact until after the race was over. And I came off not too badly at that, unless you figure that I had to give away the handicap of twenty-five years of age.

Initially I was entered in the 1984 Sydney Marathon, due to convenient scheduling and because Sydney would be my home once my wife and kids came to Australia to join me. Just before the Sydney race date, however, my co-worker in Adelaide went into the hospital with chest pains and there was nobody else available to be there as support. He turned out fine, but I stayed in Adelaide, watched the Sydney Marathon on television and looked around for another event to run instead.

The only other marathon in the offing was the Victoria State Championship Marathon in Melbourne, a smaller race three weeks away, for competitive club-level runners. This was no big-city people's event with thousands of entries. There would be a couple of hundred at most, and they would be very fast. Normal recreational runners would be left bringing up the rear alone. I called the race director and discussed the situation. Based on my marathon time at Lake Kawaguchi the previous year and a recent 10-miler in Adelaide, he agreed that I would be finishing well back in the race though definitely not last. I decided to give it a go and continued training into the approaching Australian winter.

IV

Predawn stretching in my hotel room. The radio says it was minus one degree Celsius overnight. I jog a light warmup around Fitzroy Gardens. Frost on the ground under the huge old trees. Back up to the room for more preparations – then heave a sigh and step out the door at seven-twelve a.m., thoroughly bundled up.

A red sunrise is peeking over the Dandenongs as I trot across patchy grass and around the stands of the Melbourne Cricket Ground. The frost is thick, a moon just past full hangs in the northwest sky, and nobody is stirring in the winter city morning.

As I descend the footbridge over the train tracks, two joggers stride past, too early and purposeful to be anything but warming up for this race. Heading back whence they came I arrive at the Olympic Stadium where fifty or so similar figures are moving about in the cold and semi-dark of the rear entrance. It is seven twenty-five.

The Organizer explains on the speaker that clothes bags have not yet arrived, but nobody is in a hurry to take off sweats half an hour before the start. As the minutes tick by I jog around the 1956 Olympic track, now slightly dog-eared and patched, and stretch by the side of the stands. The invited Japanese runner, also named Kawaguchi, sprints up and down the main stretch at an impressive pace, getting ready to knock out five-minute miles from the starting gun.

Eventually it is seven-fifty and time to move across the Yarra River to the start. Betting that the air will warm up, or that I will, I opt for only a singlet and cotton gloves after noting a few others dressed similarly. There is little wind, but the air is icy. As we walk over the Swan Street Bridge there are fewer than three hundred other runners. A timer mounted on a car roof arrives and parts the crowd. The timer says "0" but it could also be a thermometer.

The gun goes off and we head through a tunnel to City Road and out to Port Melbourne. I am immediately far back in the race but not at the back of the pack. Struggling to keep to my own pace, I find the first mile gone by in 7:08. I expected 7:30. I decide on twenty-three minutes per five kilometers as a reasonable pace without working out quite what it means as a full course time (3:14). I expect to fade inevitably in the last segments, as I did in Japan.

As the five-kilometer segments begin to roll by, I find I am comfortably coming in thirty to sixty seconds under the twenty-three-minute target. So much the better – hang on to those minutes if possible until the late stages. After a loop around the river bend we come out onto the bay front. Nearly half the course is here, ten kilometers down and back along the water. Mercifully, the driving northwest wind I faced in practice out here a week ago is absent, and I hope it remains so – the return half of the bay leg is straight into the northwest.

I talk to a heavy runner whose father just died this past Thursday. His father had fought alongside Americans at Guadalcanal. I run alongside a kid whose teacher is in the pack of four leading the race. At about 1:12 into the race that pack comes flying back past us having already reached the turnaround. The kid sets a good, quick pace and I decide to stay with him as far as the turnaround if I can.

Several times I notice TV news crews ahead of me, but each time I approach their spot, they start packing up their equipment and move on. I'd love to be on the news, but I'm never close enough to the camera. Someone else will have the honor today, unless he or she tires and allows me to catch up. As we fly past the twenty-kilometer mark and into the turnaround, I am aware that this is the fastest I have ever run that distance, yet I feel fine.

The trip back up the bay finds runners spread out, silent, working to maintain pace. Nearing the thirty-kilometer mark and the end of the waterfront, immigrants selling oranges on the dock squint at the passing runners. "You tired?" croaks one, an old man. Each water break on the course is a comforting array of smiles, cups held out, cold sponges (at this temperature? You must be joking!) and a bucket to lob the cup into when done.

By thirty kilometers I am four minutes ahead of the twenty-three-minutes-per-five-kilometer pace, and resolve to hold my pace through forty kilometers if I can, instead of just to thirty-five. But the long empty streets of the Port seem to lengthen before me and by the thirty-five kilometer mark I have given back four seconds. Soon the course rounds an old yellow "hotel" (pub) and heads back northeast into the sun towards the city center. An old traffic cop advises, "Two and a half kilometers to go," but I know better. From that point it's more like four, and I tell him so. Bad advice like that doesn't help. As the course passes the Mobil Building and enters the tunnel back to the park I feel I am almost there. But the forty-kilometer sign is not where I expect it to be, and I am struggling to keep on top of the pace, actually deteriorating into a jog, leaning ahead on legs that don't have much reach in them. Finally forty kilometers appears, but my concentration is breaking. I have given back another fifty-two seconds to the pace, but there are only two kilometers and a little more to go. I take a last cup of water, walk past the table to the bucket, pitch it in and set off towards the bridge.

As I approach the bridge over the Yarra back to the stadium, something else is wrong. There are no runners on the road on the other side, and I know there should be several in sight ahead of me. Struggling up to bridge level is like hauling myself out of a swimming pool without a ladder. Now I see that the course continues on straight from the bridge into the city, rather than turning left – it will be longer back to the stadium than I thought. The route goes onto a sidewalk past the Armory, then bends left to make a circuit the long way around the block. This wasn't on the course map. Unprepared for the deviation and unsure of how far I have to go, I can push on but the urge to stride to the finish is gone. Disheartened, I walk a few steps, then a few more. I have come too far to end like this, however, and force myself to lurch into a semblance of a run. After six hundred meters of city sidewalk we turn a sharp left and there is the finish banner. Now the will returns and I am able to pass one runner on the way up to the chute. Punching the button on my watch as I finally stop, I reflect how much shorter this race seemed than my first one.

It was shorter, by twenty-one minutes. I did pass maybe twenty-five runners in the last half of the race, and held my pace well past thirty-five kilometers. One I didn't pass was a big guy with a lurching gait, wearing Australian Flag–patterned shorts and loudly thanking every policeman on every corner. There is a character at the finish I wish I could have a picture of – track suit, bush boots, a "digger" hat over a sunbrowned face, and a white scraggly beard.

After the race it is necessary to keep moving to keep warm, but also progressively more difficult as muscles begin to stiffen. I recall that I could barely move thirty minutes after my first marathon, and as soon as they announce the winners I begin walking back to the hotel (Graeme Kennedy is first in 2:14:16, Kawaguchi is second twenty-five seconds back, and the kid's teacher, Chris Lynch, is fourth in 2:18.)

Nobody is selling hot drinks at the stadium. I buy, therefore, an ice cream cone – on Melbourne's coldest day of the year. Another hundred yards along, my left calf cramps so badly I have to stop and sit on the low pipe fence. Soon another runner, with wife and two boys 14 and 9 for support, offers me a ride back. With a few painful halts I reach their van – and wonder upon wonders, *they* have hot tomato soup! The boys tell me who's good in the Footy leagues this year. Their dad ran a 2:40 today, also his best by far. Probably a lot of people have set personal records today. Too soon, we're at the hotel and I thank them wholeheartedly and hobble in. Such kindness to a stranger.

My time of 3:13:29, it turns out, was just five places behind Cliff Young. The thought kind of puts things in perspective. Cliff Young, the winner of last year's Melbourne-to-Sydney race and a household word in running circles here, came in at 3:11:25. This was the reason that the television crews were out on the waterfront, just pulling up their mikes and cameras as I got to them, because Cliff Young had just passed. That man has run races over six hundred miles long. He could probably just as well run home to his farm from the finish while I'm creaking back to take a nap in my hotel. But for the rest of my life I will have the honor of having finished just two minutes behind Cliff Young in a distance race.

Overall, it is also noteworthy that for the only time in my life, I have finished within an hour (by 47 seconds) of the winner. On the other hand, equally unusually, I am in the second half of the finishers in this very fast field, having come in 150th out of 258. Still, I take quiet pride that I have run with a fast group of Australia's better amateur distance runners and, for one day at least, did not do badly at all.

The Victoria State Championship Marathon remains my all-time fastest by a wide margin. Ten years would pass before I ran another marathon, and only once, in 1995, would I again come within ten minutes of the time I ran in Melbourne.

V

George Sheehan quotes the child psychologist Joan Cass as saying that play is a child's assurance of immortality. The child within us, in play, acts out self-created dramas including not only victory but hard knocks and pain as well. The child knows that it is playing, and yet is capable of taking play very seriously.[5] The Australians I ran with demonstrated a deep appreciation for play as essential in life, an appreciation for the drama that play creates as well as the value of participating. There is a lesson somewhere in these experiences, about how to take life.

One has to love the extra effort Australians make to ensure that competition is fair and fun, that as many participate as possible and have a good time, and that exertion in sports is seen as a normal, natural part of life. The Sydney Corporate Cup continues to this day though the format has changed somewhat, and though I have long since left that company, I would love to run through the green of the Domain to the Opera House and back again. Something tells me, however, that they still have my 27:40 handicap time on file and I know I won't be scoring any points now, twenty years later. Don't bet on me. I don't crawl up windowpanes as well as I used to, mate.

---

[5] George Sheehan, *Going the Distance: one man's journey to the end of his life*. New York, Villard, 1996, pp. 63-65.

Book Bag

Light, entertaining material for an understanding of the
Australian experience as seen through Australian eyes:

Henry Lawson, *While the Billy Boils, Joe Wilson's Mates,* and
other short stories.

Jeanie (Mrs. Aneas) Gunn, *We of the Never-Never.*

Colin Thiele, *Storm Boy*

A. B. "Banjo" Patterson, *Collected Poems*

Classic films: *Gallipoli (1981), The Sundowners (1960),
Storm Boy (1976), Sunday Too Far Away (1975)*

Antarctica

Gentoo penguins on the way to the water, Couverville Island.

The Last Marathon
Bellingshausen Station, King George Island,
Antarctica
February 1997

Southern
Ocean

King George
Island

Collins
Glacier

▲ 679   ▲ 660

Admiralty
Bay

▲ 173
Arctowsky
(POL)

Artigas (URU)
Bellingshausen
(RUS)
Marsh (Chile)
Great Wall
(China)

▲ 232

▲ 275

▲ 345

▲ 196

▲ 60

▲ 7

▲ 94

Nelson
Island

Bransfield
Strait

King George
Island

N
W — E
S

Antarctica

ANTARCTICA:
The route of the 1997 Last Marathon on King George Island, Antarctica. The race started and ended at Bellingshausen Station (Russia), with one trip up the Collins Glacier, another as far as Artigas Station (Uruguay), and three trips through Marsh Station (Chile) to Great Wall Station (China) and back.

CHAPTER 4

Summer at the End of the World

Antarctica, February 1997

Whenever I find myself growing grim about the
mouth; whenever it is a damp, drizzly November in
my soul;…. I account it high time to get to sea as soon
as I can…If they but knew it, almost all men in their
degree, some time or other, cherish very nearly the same
feelings towards the ocean with me.

Herman Melville, *Moby Dick, or The*
Whale, Chapter 1, "Loomings"

My anthropologist wife is succinct. "You're crazy. There's no human society down there at all!" She is correct. Also, these are the main reasons why I am going. For most of eternity, the waves journey across the stones. Once in a while it's time for a stone to travel over the waves.

SUNDAY, FEBRUARY 9, 1997 — DEPARTURE

Like Melville's Ishmael, I go to church before embarking. The pastor spots me in the balcony and announces my trip, though I twice have discouraged him from doing so. The pastor himself is going to Cambodia again this week – a journey of more significance, driven by compassion, demanding no less endurance than mine. He is taking prosthetic arms and legs for victims of landmine explosions. He has done this before, and will again. It occurs to me that he too might like to be headed away from human society at times.

The van ride to the airport is chatty, euphoric. Ray, the driver, asks me to take a front seat so he won't have to sit next to the other passenger who "smokes like a chimney." At the airport, where others sit at tables with burritos, juice and boredom, I test human society by asking the next table to watch my bag while I go to get a salad. In shocked tones, one man emphatically refuses, "If security comes by, I'd have to tell them it wasn't mine." He has the tone of one challenging a supervisor. Good for him...this is 1997 and the times have changed.

Ishmael normally sailed aboard merchant vessels, worked a few voyages and returned ashore. But once for some reason he chose to ship out on a whaler and the result was *Moby Dick*. Life in the company of red-meat hunters from places as far as the South Seas and as near as Connecticut became the genesis of an epic sea tale, a journey to the depth of the ocean, the seat of God, and a sermon on the meaning of life itself. The Antarctic has been the destination of some of the greatest adventurers in history, Amundsen, Scott, Shackleton, Palmer in past years, and others yet living and perhaps still working on the White Continent.

Why would anyone head for those harsh, remote, alien shores? Why put down a perfectly good book about Shackleton, lift the eyes from Frank Hurley's legendary photographs of the *Endurance* buckling in the pack ice, and actually assemble gear to undertake a journey there? Existence in damp, drizzly Oregon has become familiar and confined, and for several years, running has been the primary means of navigating my regular storms of disquietude. To run is simultaneously to fight and to flee, also a chance to think and dream and yet prove the ultimate truth of one's existence in the slap and push of feet against gravity and the grit of the trail. Perhaps I want to do these things to a far greater degree than my fellow runners, even those who are tangibly driven, lemming-like, by the same emotions.

Why not run at the end of the earth? It is no longer the age of sail, when wooden hulls had to contend with sharp-edged ice and rely on vicious winds for power. The early explorers truly extended the edge of the possible, though I will ship as a passenger, ride on a research ship built for Antarctic waters, and am pursuing legends that perhaps exist in my mind alone. I want to set foot on the Antarctic continent, fix my eyes on its ice and wildlife for as long as they will stay open, see the world-class geological wonder of Deception Island and if possible enter its active caldera. To touch the end of the world but that is not only possible but safe. Mad captains are not in the plan. I want to photograph whales, not harpoon them. I will tackle the marathon for the sixth time, but will have as much time as I need and no message to deliver at the finish. On board will be dozens of others there for the same purpose, but they may have no more insight than I as to why. If I am not doing this just for show, it will be up to me to prove this to myself. The meaning of life may reveal itself, but it will be up to me to spot it.

Great and small travelers pass through Los Angeles International Airport, faces arriving from Connecticut passing others headed for Pacific islands. So many people wear running shoes that it's hard to pick out the runners at my departure gate. Two young Argentine men are loaded down with half a dozen tennis rackets each. One guy is wearing a Honolulu Marathon baseball cap. A large family of perhaps ten Japanese includes three generations, many in running gear. Then I do overhear two Antarctic-bound runners discovering each other, and we spend the next hour chatting.

Takeoff is smooth, and soon the LA basin slips beneath us, an orange curtain drawing aside to disclose the marine night. Ahead in 7 hours 45 minutes we will touch down at Lima, Peru. The Argentine chief purser is smiley and cordial. He lets the women do the work. Dinner is airline chicken for the second time today, and sleep follows, for a while.

By 7:00 Lima time (4:00 a.m. at home) the smallest member of the Japanese family is stirring. She wails "mama iya" (mommy, no) over and over loudly and wakes much of the cabin. Volcanic cones loom on the eastern horizon as a distant red sun grows behind them. This could be southern Mexico, El Salvador, Costa Rica. I pace the cabin for 45 minutes, get cups of bottled water from the galley, then clip the map from the flight magazine. It has interesting, Argentine place names, including a part of the Southern Ocean called "Mar de Franklin Roosevelt."

Coastal South America appears with the morning. Dusty-looking deserts are broken by dry rivers and occasional steep, sere mountains. What country is this? Ecuador or Peru, probably, I expected forested mountains like in the pictures of Machu Picchu, and maybe snowy peaks. But this looks bone dry and severely hot. The mountains grow higher, brown and rough, broken by a multitude of parched valleys. The rivers all run west and look dry. There is some sign of trees just below the clouds at higher elevations in the distance but the nearer valleys are in sepia tones, subtle browns and dun-colors in the river beds of sand.

The baby squalls. We are descending.

Lima airport is brown and dusty, like its surroundings. A transit lounge has shops with alpaca sweaters and neo-Inca jewelry, and little else to do but swelter. But then I meet Johnny Johnson.

Dressed in shorts and a spanking new Air Force cap, he looks like a small, bright-eyed retiree on a vacation. With much of the transit lounge empty, Johnny sits right down next to me and starts his story. He's going back from Lima to Buenos Aires to continue a trip from Australia to Miami (figure that...), and has been in 104 countries, 90 since 1991 if I have it right. And he has a small album with one photo from each country. But this voyager (says he's a security "consultant" at U.S. embassies) doesn't just take any old snapshots, or travel the shortest routes. His pictures of Norway are in Spitsbergen, of Tanzania are Victoria Falls, of Kenya a highland Masai school. Also in the album are Medan, Sumatra...North Vietnam...Angkor Wat, Cuzco, the Plain of Jars (Laos), more predictably the Great Wall of China, St. Basil's in Moscow...some kind of tourist! In the back he has photos of himself with Bill Clinton (both first and second term) and other notables including Aun San Soo Kyi at her home in Burma, where she lives under house arrest. My own destination, purpose, motives, even my need to tell about them, are not to be compared with those of this ancient mariner and I am quickly spellbound.

Another boarding call is given, and the flight from Lima to Buenos Aires is cloudy except for glimpses of Peruvian coastline (sun, surf and more dust) and some Argentine farmland (the squares are very large). The TV shows highlights from an under-20 youth soccer tournament. The passengers cheer as Argentina beats Brazil 2-0, then shake heads when Chile scores a bad goal against Paraguay. A gruesomely violent action film follows. I have my running shoes, jacket, notebooks with me in the cabin and wonder whether the rest of my luggage is in the hold.

Buenos Aires comes in sight, a broad expanse of white towers lit by the late afternoon sun, standing out against dark green carpet. The city must be of white and light gray concrete, and it is all lit by the western sun. The land around is as flat and cultivated as Iowa. I am conscious of approaching one of the great cities of the world.

Landing is without incident (if you ignore the ancient smashed-up fuselage beside one runway), the small child bawling again, clearing its ears in a final aria. I see cars; they drive on the right side of the road here. The airport is white, modern, petite. The climate is deliciously late summer, leafy and lazy, the smell of new-mown lawns and barbecue in the February air. Marathon Tours has a bus at the ready, and our Antarctic group assembles and defines itself. A group from Japan – after years of living in that country I feel at home in their language, and make an introduction. Several have just run the Las Vegas Marathon – yesterday! They finished just hours before boarding for Buenos Aires and must have slept well. One is a wizened veteran of many races including the 99th and 100th Boston Marathon, and "will do the 101st." Kids play soccer in parks along the highway.

The Intercontinental Hotel is cosmopolitan and could be anywhere in the world. I meet my roommate, Kevin. I am not traveling with a casual outdoorsman. He's on a three-month paid sabbatical from an executive marketing job, started by kayaking in Baja, then climbed Aconcagua and spent a week rafting and fishing in Patagonia (never less than 20 fish a day, rainbows and browns up to 22 inches and three pounds). He'll go on from here to New Zealand, Bora Bora and Tahiti. He also looks like he's in terrific shape.

At cocktails, rosters are posted by flight time and running event. At this point 98 runners are here, including 92 signed up for the marathon. At my table are Willard from Wyoming, Mohamed from Baltimore, Huck from California. Thom Gilligan, the organizer, speaks at length about environmental impact and publicity from the last event, which has been unfavorably and inaccurately reflected in the Lonely Planet travel guides.

The first rule is respect for the environment, never to approach marine wildlife, remove any objects, or step off established paths. The ships have been flip-flopped; I will be on the *Sergei Vavilov* instead of the *Ioffe*. The ship and crew are Russian and on shipboard Russian rules apply as well. Never shake hands across a door-sill, instead step through the door first. Do not whistle aboard the ship; whistling brings bad weather. Where we are going, the weather can get very bad indeed.

Also, the President of Uruguay has picked our scheduled race day, February 18, to visit his base, which was to have acted as host for our race. We will have to work around that. The *Ioffe* will depart two days later and will be the more inconvenienced, having less time. Wait and see. Reliable weather forecasts are not available. The rule of travel in Antarctica is to "expect changes of plans at all times."

My bags not yet having arrived at the room, I am still in a blue wrinkle-proof sport coat with many pockets, great for travel, but I'd like to change. Hopefully this coat will pay off when traveling in Argentina on the way back. The locals seem friendly, but I have found that plain respectful address goes a long way. I use Spanish phrases when I can but I have such a long way to go in this culture. Being able to use a few words in Argentina doesn't really break the ice the way it can in Asia – there you get points for trying. Here I feel you don't get any points at all unless you can say it correctly *and* with style.

My roommate, as well as Johnny Johnson and even my pastor back home, is showing me that I have a long way to go as a world traveler. I am being reminded that I have a long way to go in the running culture too, feeling outclassed by the T-shirts I see on all sides. Many of the runners are already in shirts that announce their exploits: 50-state marathoners, Western States 100-milers, veterans of obscure and distant marathons in Kenya, Nepal. It is not unlike the feeling of standing at the start of a race, among others who are the likely winners, or have more experience, or better equipment, or just a bigger group of friends. I am no beginner, however, and once one learns that the race is not always to the swift it becomes easier to focus on personal reasons for entering and running. And then eventually the starter's gun goes off and feet are set in motion and the only thing that matters is getting down the path as well as the day may allow. We are still many days from race time however. Bedtime beckons. Wakeup tomorrow is at 3:45 a.m. for a 4:30 bus to catch a 6:00 flight!

TUESDAY, FEBRUARY 11   ➔   BUENOS AIRES

The alarm goes off. The eyes protest. The hour is still 10:45 p.m. back home. After all that travel and good white wine, I could have slept for hours. There is a brightly lit buffet breakfast, runny eggs with strong coffee, croissants without number. The juice glass keeps filling itself.

The Aeroparque is like a big bus terminal, all hurry up and wait. After the ice-breaking dinner party last night, the group is comfortable but the hour is not. Takeoff is at dawn, Uruguay grayly visible in the distance over the Rio de la Plata as we bank and wheel back over the city. The land is flat, flat, flat. The river is named "flat" (what big river isn't flat?). Then the solar glare and haze obscure the Mar de Plata in the east, and after about an hour we pass over a beach of grassy dunes and out over the water. Today's second breakfast arrives with more croissants.

Across from me is Barry, a self-employed Australian with a background in printing technology. We have enough in common and talk our way south through the three-hour flight. At length the plane reaches another coast line, then abruptly there are high snow-capped peaks and we descend over a long east-west channel slashing between them; the Beagle Passage in Tierra del Fuego. The plane executes a 270° turn over the channel as the passengers buzz with interest. The landing is to the east on an island projecting into the channel.

With a bump we are in Ushuaia, now looking up at craggy peaks and glacial valleys reminiscent of Banff in Canada. The plane taxis up to a spiffy new ski-lodge–like terminal. It is not yet open, however, and we are bused slowly around gritty military barricades and water-filled ditches to an old dumpy terminal building several miles away. The town stretches up the hills and a few big buildings are visible very high up. We beat the luggage to the Hotel Des Glacieres above the town, then find that a large group is in the process of leaving and we have to wait until nearly 12:30 to get our rooms. I battle the temptations of sleepiness and the gift shop and lose on both counts.

Once in the room, I am no longer sleepy. The phone works; I get Nancy at home just as our youngest is leaving for school. The call is over too soon, and we will be out of telephone contact from now on, until we sight each other in Buenos Aires in two

weeks. Can't sleep now...the sun is partially out and several runners are striding up the road behind us to the glacier, or down
the hillside to the town. I have another plan, pack the tripod
and cameras up there and practice shooting with the lenses and
filters. There is a path into the woods west of the hotel that yields
some close-ups of moss and streams. The rest of that walk is on
film. Ascending the glacier valley as high as necessary to take
a shot of the town and channel, I then find that the real story
is in miniature right at my feet, in the rocks and moss of a wet
alpine meadow. I choose to ride down the ski lift before it closes
for the afternoon. Back at the hotel by 5:00, I have time for a
half-hour run back up the road and then return for dinner. Sleep
is delicious, ten hours without a dream.

Wednesday, February 12 ⬤ Ushuaia

Morning. Kevin arrived on a late plane yesterday and skips the
National Park tour to take the city bus and go trout fishing again.
The tour is an hour late starting but is worth it once we are in
the park. The bus stops at Ensenada Bay, shale outcroppings
around a grassy bay on the Beagle Channel. There are three
species of tree...and only three...for hundreds of miles around.
All members of the "fagus" family, these are called (Patagonian)
southern beeches and resemble firs from a distance but two types
are deciduous and the third evergreen. Fossil remnants of these
trees are found in Antarctica. Other plants at the bay include a
holly and a type of sage. We have time to hike through wooded
areas and a meadow down to another overview of the channel,
this time looking westward to the Pacific. A small oceangoing
yacht is coming in under a French flag. Here too are middens left
by the Yamani culture, short sturdy people who fed on shellfish
and marine life. It is also the end of the Pan-American Highway,
complete with a "Photo-op" sign saying that Alaska is 17,800
km away.

We go by bus straight to the pier. The *Vavilov* is there, taller, longer and sturdier than I expected. That's very good. Barry and his Australian group shipped out yesterday on a much smaller vessel. Today they are out on the high seas. After short trips to a grocery (gumdrops, champagne) and an Antarctic museum (postcards, patches, stamps) and post office, I stroll out in time to see a Honda 4-wheel ATV loaded aboard the ship – probably for the marathon support crew.

There is nothing left to do on shore. Ahead, the sea. Up the gangway, and into a clean, brightly lit corridor trimmed in light wood. People in red cotton shirts with Marine Expeditions logos are everywhere. My passport and plane ticket are surrendered to the steward and I check into Room 302, just around the corner. All the halls are equally spotless, light wood railings everywhere. After a few mistakes such as wandering into the crew's quarters downstairs where the names are all in Russian, I find there are six levels. The third, where I am staying, has the dining hall and passenger mud room for hosing down after landings, and is the lowest level with an outdoor deck. I am really in a convenient place. The fourth and fifth levels are the main cabin floors and exit to outdoor decks at different points. The sixth deck has the bridge and lecture hall, and one can even climb to the roof above that.

Welcome drinks and orientation are served at 5:00 p.m. We are still at the pier but soon move out to the fueling station nearby to take on bunker fuel, a slow process that takes a couple of hours. The ship finally sails around 8:00 as we are sitting down to dinner, served by the Russian staff. There is a cardboard cutout of the ship in the corridor with snapshots and names of all the crew, who are Russians from Kaliningrad (Konigsberg). The people from Marine Expeditions are responsible for the tour agenda other than the marathon, and are multinational. Having gotten us on board, Marathon Tours is now only responsible for the race.

The lifeboat drill is sobering. No one wants any part of being in the Southern Ocean. The lifeboats themselves are closed-top cylinders like soup cans. Thirty is a crowd in there, though capacity is listed as sixty. The only means of propulsion is a little auxiliary diesel engine that sits right in the compartment with us, and has a manual starting crank. We are adventurers on an adventure, and it's nice to know the boats are there but I'll admit to dreading the thought that anybody might ever have to use them.

To underscore that thought, the evening film presentation is about Ernest Shackleton and the crew of the *Endurance*, one of the greatest of adventures. We will be in the same waters that Shackleton crossed in an open boat with seven men, trusting only that his knowledge of the currents and winds would land them at South Georgia over a thousand miles away. Every one of his crew, plus the photographic plates of photographer Frank Hurley, was eventually rescued from Elephant Island. Returning to human society in 1916, they found England at war. A number of these Antarctic survivors went on fight and die in the trenches of France.

The *Vavilov* has big diesel engines and computerized stabilizing systems, and is much larger than Shackleton's craft. The topic of conversation however is seasickness. We are told that the ship can still roll many degrees and recover, that the stabilizers are effective against repeated rolling but not necessarily perfect. We are warned to always keep a hand free to grasp a rail in case of a sudden roll. Dramamine is the drug of choice; everyone is getting very drowsy. Wrist bands are scoffed at by some but most of the passengers have theirs on, including me. The captain is asked about his favorite preventive and replies in one word, "Brandy." The word is that we will drop the pilot and leave the Beagle Channel around midnight. After that the fun will start, for the Drake Passage is the roughest ocean in the world. I sleep as if drugged, which is precisely what I am. I wake at 4:00 and feel the ocean moving beneath the floor as I take two more Dramamine. It's not too bad, hope it stays that way.

THURSDAY, FEBRUARY 13 — AT SEA

The morning sun is high, and so am I. All the world is a rolling surface, seen from up on the bridge of the *Vavilov* before breakfast, with little or no queasy feeling. The bridge is open to all passengers day or night for us to visit, observe, ask questions if we can, or just enjoy the view, by hospitable policy of the captain. All we must do is stay out of the way of the crew, and leave if we are asked to do so. It's the perfect place to observe, a wide room spanning the front of the ship from one side to the other, large thick windows around the front and sides. Inside there are instruments, radar screens, the ship's wheel, a digital compass and a TV monitor showing latitude, longitude, speed, wind speed and direction, ocean temperature and salinity and plenty else that I cannot decipher. There are also flags of all nations neatly stored in cubbyholes labeled in Cyrillic script, and a chart table where the mate marks our position every few minutes using calipers and a ruler. The *Vavilov* was built to be a research ship for the Soviet Academy of Sciences and carries a part of that body's proud tradition. The crew, we are told, are mostly science graduates and much of the ship's scientific gear is still on board where it is safer than it might be in storage somewhere.

All of that is fascinating but so is the view outside – albatrosses soaring behind and beside the ship, occasionally other birds moving across our path navigating on their way to somewhere out of sight. The sea is pretty calm, especially given the fearsome reputation of the Drake Passage.

The mood is euphoric. There may only be five albatrosses to look at, but we are all looking at them and trying the occasional long camera shot when one comes close enough. The birds seem to know just where camera range is and stay a little beyond it, then make a beautiful close loop around the front of the ship just when you go inside for coffee. They are effortless fliers, often trailing one wing just an inch above the waves to ride on the air resistance there. This allows them to disappear from our sight while scooting through wave troughs, to reappear suddenly as the next swell changes the view.

Breakfast is buffet style. The talk is all about how smooth the sea is. Some are already taking off wristbands, discontinuing

Dramamine, declaring themselves "drug-free. I join this group as of 8:00. No more seasickness for me, time to get some sea legs. This proves a little more difficult in practice. Other runners are of similar mind, holding on to hallway railings, pretending to be more balanced than we really are. The *Vavilov* is a modern research ship, built with stabilizing tanks fore and aft, starboard and port, and a computerized system that detects rolling patterns and rapidly pumps water among the tanks so as to counteract any repeated rolling motion. Every now and then the ship rolls hard in one direction or another but before a second roll can start we feel the stabilizing mechanism kick in to damp the motion and the ship sits still. The larger swells may be three stories in height but the ship takes them very smoothly and the sense of motion is exciting.

We are at sea all day today, and won't hit land until Friday afternoon. It's a good time for initial talks by our three naturalists, Stan, Giles, and Robin. Stan talks about glaciers. He's a Scotsman, taciturn, full of information but sometimes needing the right question to get going. Giles is a French Canadian geologist, with joie de vivre and a good sense of humor, much more loquacious and a veteran lecturer on cruises. He too seems to have a boundless store of information on the Antarctic. Robin, a marine wildlife specialist, has recently been bitten by a fur seal. This battle scar gives him credibility among the passengers but has also left him with a nasty bacterial infection that has not cleared up despite several months of antibiotic treatment. This is a warning to all; we must keep well away from fur seals.

Shipboard protocol is that we do not go into the personal territory of the crew, who live their lives in deck 2 and below except for the captain and chief officers, who have quarters right behind the bridge on deck 6. Deck 3 has the dining hall and we are free to sit there except when the crew has their meals, which is generally about an hour and a half before each of our own meals or just about when we would feel like sitting around there. The view isn't great through the portholes on this deck though, so in fact not much sitting takes place there except after dark when there are card games and a cash bar. Just aft of the dining hall is a wide crosswise passage with bulletin boards where information and maps are posted. Aft of that are the lower-cost cabins including mine, with men's and women's bath facilities down the hall. Still further aft are the mud room and doors out to the rear deck, a working area that extends all the way to the stern. This is the largest outdoor area on the ship, and here you can stand at the stern rail and watch where you've been while the wake churns up right beneath your feet. The deck surfaces are bright green and textured to prevent slipping. Everything else is painted white.

Decks 4 and 5 have cabins with soft chairs, some with bunks, the better ones with twin beds placed at right angles. A library is at the forward end of deck 5 with a selection of novels and books about the Antarctic, many evidently left by passengers on previous trips. It has no copy of *Moby Dick*; I will leave mine here for posterity. Exits aft lead to areas above the rear deck, connected by stairs and railings, offering a higher position from which to look to the side and behind the ship. Deck 5 also has a small pool filled with unheated sea water straight out of the ocean, for Russian style plunges after emerging from the ship's sauna.

On Deck 6 the bridge is the place to be, with windows all across the front and sides and a commanding view. Sliding doors on the port and starboard ends open to outdoor walkways. In general, the easiest place to be out of doors is alongside the bridge on whichever side is out of the wind. There is room for ten or twelve people here, if you stand close, and it's an excellent place to get the feel of the wind and the ocean, scan the horizon or watch an albatross. Aft on Deck 6 is an assembly room for lectures and instructional meetings prior to making landings. An outside staircase leads further up, onto the roof of the bridge. This is the highest vantage point, normally quite windy when the ship is under way but still a wonderful place to look out in all directions. Being the farthest point above the center of gravity, it also tosses more than anywhere else when the ship is rolling.

By dinner time, with little else to do but explore the ship, absorb lectures and feel excited about where we are going, we are feeling at home and anticipating the crossing of the Antarctic Convergence, a meeting of ocean waters south of which the climate will be considerably colder. The seventy or so passengers are beginning to know each other, but slowly. Perhaps it is my perspective but each person on this journey seems to be cloaked in his or her own expectation of deep adventure, to be undergoing the same discovery of sea, ship, wind, and motion, perhaps working through inner reasons for embarking that are more significant than human social contact at this moment.

Dinner is thick Russian stews, substantial bread, irresistible desserts. Appetites at sea really grow, we are told, yet few people gain weight. The shipboard diet has more meat than some are used to, but also plenty of the carbohydrates that marathoners gobble in great quantities. The idea of a marathoner's appetite actually increasing even further at sea is impressive. We will eat very well on this trip.

Small clusters of people with similar interests are forming. Most of the Japanese passengers group together, and some of the veteran runners start a cribbage game. A younger group plays music tapes in the dining area and asks if chairs can be moved for dancing. No, is the answer, because they are bolted to the floor for a good reason. The innocent request underscores how calmly we have crossed the notorious Drake Passage on the southbound trip.

FRIDAY, FEBRUARY 14, VALENTINE'S DAY ⟶ ANTARCTIC WATERS

No early rising today, in fact up just in time for breakfast. The food yesterday was too rich, perhaps a nice problem to have in such a remote part of the world. The talk about appetites at sea was interesting, but with a race to run in several days I resolve to stick to the things I normally eat if possible.

We crossed the Antarctic Convergence, the point where the waters of the Southern Ocean meet the waters of the Atlantic, at 4:02 this morning. There were shipboard bets placed on the time. In these food-rich waters there are suddenly many more petrels and penguins in the water, occasionally seals, and rumors of whales. Robin talks in the morning about marine mammals.

The sky is lowering, foggy and clammy, noticeably colder. We are pushing steadily south through Antarctic waters in scenery that recalls Masefield's "gray mist on the sea's face and a gray dawn breaking." The first destination will be Arctowsky Station, one of several bases on King George Island. During the morning most of us are on the bridge or decks, straining for a glimpse of each passing critter. The Drake Passage may be renowned for its powerful winds and waves but for us the crossing has actually been quite pleasant. Eventually tabular icebergs are seen, flat pieces of shelf ice low in the water. Then there is one taller berg, a chunk broken off of a glacier and now looking small in the wide seascape.

At midday the *Vavilov* rounds the tip of King George Island and enters the Bransfield Passage, a broad channel sheltered between the South Shetland Islands on the west and the Antarctic Peninsula on the east. For the next six days and nights the sailing will be calm.

After lunch there is a briefing on the international tourist guidelines. Stay fifteen feet from penguins, fifty feet from fur seals (which bite and can outrun a human). We learn procedures for the mud room and for getting into Zodiacs (inflatable landing craft) and thence to shore. Since this is the first landing, the mud room is still clean, but we will be walking through penguin colonies (guano) and mud, and our boots are to be removed and remain in the mud room for the duration of the trip. They may be hosed down but the waste water will not be discharged by the ship until it returns to South America.

My landing group of ten persons is #3. The honor of being first to depart will be rotated. The procedure is to exit through the outer door of the mud room, keep one hand on the rail when going from deck down the gangway stairs to the Zodiac, then give a "sailor's grip" to the Zodiac driver, step on the pontoon, and sit where directed, holding the rope.

The ship passes along the coast of King George Island, past high blocky capes standing out from glaciers like huge black boots. There are two icebergs, deep blue, against the coast of the first bay. Eventually the headland called Lion's Rump is sighted, smaller than I expected from the maps but resembling a prone lion facing the island. The *Vavilov* slows its speed and enters Admiralty Bay, ringed by walls of broad glaciers coming down on all sides and punctuated by rocky dividing ridges and distant protruding nunataks.

Arctowsky Station, operated by the government of Poland, is on an old whaling station site. The base itself consists of several weathered modular units and shipping containers loosely organized on a dark brown rocky point in the bay. The point features one high rock topped by an aged-looking light. One by one, my group descends the gangway stairs, grasps the arm first of the bosun then of the Zodiac driver, and finds a seat on the black pontoon surface. Debarking onto a pebbly shore at the foot of the light, we are startled to find a huge seal sleeping right there, and spend several minutes eyeing a small colony of lackadaisical penguins arranged in various attitudes on the rock.

We can go strolling two ways. Left along the gravel ridge of the shore leads to a group of elephant seals lying nearly motionless except for flatulent belches and occasional flipper gesturing, and a view of three very active fur seals chasing each other around a mossy "lawn" some distance away. After perhaps ten minutes the fur seals tire of their game and slip off into the bay.

Walking back the other way we pass the scattered modules of Arctowsky itself and go out to the point where the rusting fuel tank and heavy equipment are placed. This beach offers a good view into the lobe of the bay beyond. More glaciers cover the higher land, topped by layers of old snow and brown dust with patches of white, riven here and there by chocolate-colored crevices, and culminating in a luminous blue frontal cliff where the last chunks have broken off and calved into the ocean.

I send thirteen postcards from Arctowsky to various addresses. A gift shop and post office here will deliver mail, eventually, postmarked from Polish Antarctica. We can also get our passports stamped here as a novelty. There were once sixty people at this year-round station, but now there are only eleven, of whom perhaps six or eight will winter over. They certainly can use the tourist business due to the drastic cutback of financial support from Poland. The chief of our charter operator, Marine Expeditions, is right at home here. An Argentine named Tomas, fluent in several languages, he has once over-wintered at Arctowsky on a 14-month assignment. This in itself makes him part of an elite crew of scientists and Antarctic veterans. He must know every square meter of the place.

There are poignant artifacts at the Arctowsky site that speak of loneliness and better times. The station does not appear particularly well maintained, but as yet we do not have anything to compare it to. One of the modular buildings has a northward-facing large glass window through which we can see a Christmas tree, still green in February. The sight is incongruous; how did that tree get here and where did it start its life? Tomas relates that the staff once grew tomatoes in that building. The most memorable human touch is a city bus stop sign in Polish, taken from a street in Gdansk or Warsaw and hauled all the way to this icy, rocky island and planted in the gravel bank of the bay west of the station by someone with a sense of humor and a flair for symbolism. Tomas explains that the bus stop represents the fondest wish of everyone doing an assignment at the station, to finish work, go out at quitting time and take the ride home.

The ship leaves a crate of fresh fruits and vegetables for the staff at Arctowsky as thanks for hosting us. Leaving Admiralty Bay, there are spectacular views of the glaciated shores, and many small ice bits floating in the calm water.

After leaving Arctowsky at around 7:30 that evening several of us have been standing on the bridge of the *Vavilov* with binoculars trained on the passing coast when, without warning, we are asked to leave the bridge. We follow the order without questioning, and a few minutes later as we wait for dinner, we learn the reason. Two of the passengers, Brad and Lola from Pennsylvania, were just married on the bridge at their request by Captain Beluga, with two of the older passengers witnessing on five minutes' notice. A commotion ensues at dinner, with wine for all tables and toasts all around. The Captain tells us it is the first marriage he has performed in all his years of sailing, and wishes the couple all the best, in English and Russian. Brad wears a suit coat and Lola a small bridal tiara and veil – they actually planned this! The Japanese passengers are astounded (no go-between in the ceremony, and they shared the same room!), but all aboard are impressed with this couple's sense of style.

After dinner, Thom Gilligan of Marathon Tours and three others go ashore to negotiate the marathon date and a course. The evening film is cancelled in favor of a Valentine's party, which turns out to be no more than a dozen partiers plus four cribbage players. Someone designs an Antarctic Athletic Federation tattoo and invites all to get it applied in Buenos Aires. The Japanese are astounded again.

In one day we have crossed the Antarctic Convergence, left the Drake Passage and entered Antarctic waters, landed at Arctowsky station, and even celebrated a wedding. It has been a wonderful day. There is a satisfying feeling of having arrived, of having wonderful times ahead, and of being in good company. Sleep is long and satisfying and the ship purrs further south.

Saturday, February 15 ━ Bransfield Passage

Up early before 6:00. This is too little sleep but the Antarctic summer sun is already high, illuminating a mountain and glacier vista off the starboard side that is simply awesome. I go up to the bridge, coffee in hand. An animated discussion is going on among the four Russians up there. The coast in sight is Livingston Island.

The mate taps my shoulder and says in thickly accented English "Two whales," pointing to sixty degrees off the port bow. I strain for a while to see, feeling foolish, then see first one back and another nearby. Through the binoculars the flukes are unmistakable as the whales dive. I make out humps and "knuckles" on the ridge of the back. These are humpback whales, and Robin confirms the sighting at breakfast.

The binoculars are a gift from my family. The advice on shipboard is never to go up to the bridge without binoculars or a camera, preferably both. The wisdom in this has already been confirmed and there is optical equipment around the neck of every passenger much of the day. For landings, I carry zip-lock bags in which I place my cameras and binoculars before returning to the ship. This allows them to warm up slowly without attracting condensation on the inner lens surfaces, but it also means that I am without a camera for perhaps the first hour after making a landing.

Today's first landing will be at Hannah Point on Livingston Island, a penguin, seal and seabird habitat. Robin describes it as a "zoo" where many forms of Antarctic wildlife are present in a small area, a good introduction to species and how they live. We are briefed before departure as to where we will be allowed to walk, and what we can expect to see.

Once ashore we find little space to walk once we are on shore but within this small rocky area we are able to slowly skirt penguin nests. Chinstrap penguins occupy the higher ground, gentoos lower down. Both species sometimes stand unconcerned next to each other on pebbly nests on barren rocks painted with long white streaks of their guano. Here and there, patches of bright green moss are interspersed with lichens of gold, tan and white. We know we are to avoid all mosses and lichen, stay fifteen feet away from all penguins and also to avoid all seals but that is nearly impossible for seventy-five tourists to do at the same time in this communal zoo. With much slow stepping and detouring we work around the animals and each other. On one side of the rocky point a vantage point overlooks a beach where more than a dozen elephant seals lie in a brown wallow like huge belching sausages, scratching and smelling to high heaven. Several more, including the bull, lie below a cliff on the other side of the point.

The penguins are irrepressibly social, hardly distracted by us, and genuinely entertaining. We humans are trained to get the most out of our effort, and many are snapping pictures as if this were the last opportunity we will have. High above the cliff top above us giant petrels are swooping and soaring. Their nesting grounds are off limits. Beyond the point, blue-eyed shags (cormorants) nest, and a pair of cape petrels roost high in a cleft on a rock face. All these species feed off the abundant marine life, as do the penguins. But some birds make a living from the penguin colony in other ways. White sheathbills strut around on the ground ready to steal a meal by disrupting a penguin regurgitating a meal for its chick. Large predatory gulls called skuas patrol from the air and will kill an unprotected chick. Everything feeds off something, and little is wasted. A penguin skeleton with skin attached testifies to the sharpness of the skuas' bills. It has been turned inside out and neatly picked of every tissue worth eating.

After humans and penguins have regarded each other for a couple of hours we return by Zodiac to the ship, give a "sailor's grip" to the bosun on the gangway, hose down our boots outside and remove them in the mud room. Then it's time for a delicious repast of stew and black bread.

Today shipboard life is run according to landings. No one objects when meals are rescheduled because conditions are calm enough to land at Bailey Head, a colony of 100,000 chinstrap penguins on Deception Island. There are also expected to be a number of fur seals on the beach, and as soon as we land, our affable, professorial lecturers are posted with canoe paddles to ward off any carnivore attacks. It doesn't look like it would be an equal match.

I am in the first Zodiac to land. The beach is narrow and steep. One gets out of a Zodiac by sitting on the pontoon, swinging the feet towards the stern and over into the water, which here is deep. The key is my hip boots, which handle the waves and tricky black sand beach well. Skirting the fur seal area, we work our way a pace at a time up a creek flowing brown with guano from the huge amphitheater-shaped rookery. One has to move slow and look sharp – two fur seals are patrolling on the other side of the river.

The amphitheater itself must be twice the size of the Rose Bowl, green with moss and white-brown with guano six inches or more deep in places. Penguins are everywhere. Feeding, chasing, squabbling, defending, pebble thieving, sudden outbursts of braying, and group drinking from the creek are taking place on all sides. I have brought a tripod ashore this time, and find penguin behavior being modeled on all sides of me. The rest of this story is told in several rolls of photos.

The sheer numbers of penguins combined with the fifteen-foot rule limit our incursion to a high spot on the near wall of the rookery. We are uncertain how to apply the rule if a penguin fifteen feet away decides it wants to walk across our boots. After more than an hour at Bailey Head, I am still finding penguin behavior irresistible, and I am actually the last to leave. But the ship is going to a world-class destination next, into the fascinating caldera of Deception Island. It is afternoon and still fairly bright out, though clouds are building fast.

The view from the deck is breathtaking as we enter Neptune's Bellows. The Deception Island volcano rises from the sea floor, erupts frequently, and at other times has turned the water inside its caldera to boiling temperatures. The Bellows is a narrow break in the rim. Most of the passengers and many crew are out on deck as the *Vavilov* glides between sheer walls of volcanic cliff only yards away, riding smoothly into harbor within the mountain. Inside, the weather has turned to gray clouds and impending rain.

We anchor in Whaler's Bay just inside the caldera, obviously an excellent harbor but also much studied in connection with times the volcano has erupted – and altered the bay – as recently as 1967, 1969, and 1970. On shore are an abandoned, rusting group of whaling-station buildings plus a few modular buildings that are a Chilean research station. Our Zodiac was the first ashore at Bailey Head – now we go to the end of the line.

A small Chilean naval vessel also lies at anchor. Ruined buildings are placed at odd intervals on the beach, a row of bright yellow tents farther up on the rim to the right, back towards Bailey Head. Someone, perhaps Chilean sailors, is sliding down the snowy glacier behind the buildings.

The long black sand beach is perfect for running, an appealing prospect after a few days' confinement. Most of the group opts for a walk and historical lecture from Gilles. Five or six of us. however, choose instead to jog up to the "Window," a huge opening in the caldera wall overlooking a sheer drop to the ocean outside. The view of wild waves and skies outside the wall appears only at the last moment, terrible and stunning but defying photography. It would be like trying to capture a window frame while one is standing in the window.

On the return run we pass a series of barrels arrayed like walls of a building with their hoops removed and staves burst. A loud snort startles me – there is a bull fur seal inside one – and I depart hastily. It begins to rain.

The lecture group is late returning. We huddle against a rusted metal ship, hull overturned in the sand. Two of the Russian Zodiac drivers take a paddle and dig a pit near the shore. The water that seeps in is uncomfortably hot. Most of us are planning to take the waters at Pendulum Cove on the northeast shore of the bay but a New Zealand runner who ran up to the Window with us decides to try it here and then go back to the ship. After a few tries he gets the right amount of ocean and hot water mixed and sits in the natural hot tub, making comparisons to Rotorua. It's maybe eight inches deep but definitely hot. In a few minutes he is back inside the rusted hull, changed, dry, and has "done the hot spring thing" in Antarctic waters. The Russians, in heavy boots and orange jumpsuits, stand in the seeping water warming their feet. The seventy-nine-year-old woman from Japan has stayed here too, plainly cold and ready to go back.

Finally the lecture group returns and in four Zodiacs we go on to Pendulum Cove while one Zodiac returns to the *Vavilov*. What at first was described as a nine- or ten-minute Zodiac trip to the cove grows longer. It turns out that the Zodiacs are not equal in speed, and we are in a slow one. We are not only left behind but run out of gas well away from shore. After switching to spare tanks, we arrive wetter and colder than ever, and the beach party is well in progress. The rain has let up but the sky is still low. Someone has brought a CD player with surf music. As we strip down to bathing attire in the frigid air, the mood gets raucous and silly. The sand is cold but at the shore the water is scalding for the first three feet, then abruptly turns Antarctic-cold beyond that. The trick is to mix the two to get comfortable.

Even properly mixed, the hot water is shocking. If you keep moving, it's actually pretty good for a while. I get warm, then take a run into the deeper water, dive and swim back. I have one fellow runner snap my picture as I run through the shallows and that's it for me. I decide to get dressed and for the next fifteen minutes or so use my hip boots again to good advantage, wading out to snap photos of others on their cameras. The numbers of runners in the water gradually decrease, and it is time to go.

The *Vavilov* has followed us to the cove, so it is a mercifully short Zodiac ride back to the ship. I stand at the rail, this time alone, as we sail again through the spectacular gap of the Bellows and back out into the Bransfield Passage. I go below only when the Bellows has faded from view, leaving an island I have studied and a visit I have anticipated for nearly a year. The shower and dinner are delicious, and sleep is heavy on quiet seas.

SUNDAY, FEBRUARY 16 ⚬ BRANSFIELD PASSAGE

Dawn is gray and rainy. Scheduled are visits to Half Moon and Aitcho Islands. Tomorrow is race day.

Half Moon is too cold and rainy to be much of interest. Although it is well above freezing I under-dress, and carelessly let my lenses get wet. I should know better, because the conditions are exactly like home this time of year. I can't believe I left Oregon in winter to go somewhere at the end of the world where it is 40°F in light rain. I am reduced to taking close-ups of rocks and a few forlorn penguins. The low cloud ceiling is a pity, because the map shows us surrounded by snowy island peaks around a good-sized bay. The euphoria of the past two days recedes; the "damp drizzly November" of the soul moves back in. I return early to the ship, disgusted by rainy lenses and sticking shutters, and sleep through the early afternoon as the ship moves on.

By the time of the Aitcho landing, I am just rested enough to feel like giving it a go. The weather is slightly better, not actually raining but still gray. The meal schedule is changing to accommodate the tastes of runners and we run tomorrow, so it's pasta at lunch, and more pasta to come at dinner.

Aitcho is a group of islands. We are to land at one, and make a leisurely walk over the hill to another beach where the Zodiacs will meet us. It will be good to have a short hike. I put on more clothes than at Half Moon, and the scenery is well worth the effort. There are sharp pinnacles and fins of rock in the bay to the north that resemble the Chinese landscape paintings of Kweilin. The moss is bright green, like a picture of Ireland. Penguins strut and fuss, seals wallow and sleep, skuas wheel overhead and scheme. It's already becoming a familiar pattern. We have to zig and zag to avoid mossy areas. The mud is seriously deep. Again I witness penguin chicks being fed regurgitated krill, only a few steps away from me. The trail we have hiked winds down to a pretty, semi-circular beach and the Zodiacs are waiting.

It is a short cruise back to King George Island, during which we runners pack in quantities of pasta. Well after dark we drop anchor and pick up Thom Gilligan at the Russian base, named Bellingshausen. He has set up the course, and is eager to eat and talk at the same time. There is a problem with the loop-course approach. The back side of the island is far too muddy this year. We will have to run a double out-and-back, to the Collins Glacier at one end and the Chinese base at the other. There is mud everywhere. For the umpteenth time we are warned to take the race slowly. We retire for the night amid much anticipation. The *Ioffe* left Ushuaia two days after us, and is due to arrive in the bay overnight with the other group of runners.

Monday, February 17 — Race Day — Bellingshausen Base

The weather has changed overnight. Fresh *snow* lies on all the visible hills and a stiff thirty-knot wind is blowing. The wind is coming straight in from 114 degrees southeast, a neat trick because that is exactly the heading into this long well-sheltered anchorage, the harbor for four research bases. We were told to expect the unexpected, and this day will bear out that advice.

Zodiac boarding is delayed, then the decision is made to go. The ride in is long, really rough, and wet with the wind and waves at our backs. I have with me all the running gear I could use, two water bottles (the other two are supposed to be set out by the glacier at Artigas, the Uruguayan base) and warm clothes for afterward. I can't drink too much beforehand, because there are said to be no toilets ashore. That is an incongruous way to start a marathon, but we are here for a challenge. The choice of shoes is also an interesting problem. Some will wear heavier, more waterproof shoes but the added weight will make a difference. I choose a pair of Asics running shoes that have high rubber siding and relatively little cloth. I have an old pair of light, comfortable Epirus Classics in reserve and hope I don't have to use them. There will be a number of stream crossings but I'll have to see them to know how bad they really are.

We land on the rocky beach at Bellingshausen and gather in the large dilapidated movie room. It's too cold to run in shorts as I had wanted. Yesterday that would have worked. Today it's still 3°C or 38°F but the persistent thirty-knot wind promises a nasty wind chill factor. Oh well, you wanted to run in Antarctica....

The race plans go very much awry. The *Ioffe's* Zodiacs cannot land in the high waves and their captain has called them back to the ship. (Later I will hear that even the runners in the first boat agreed this was the correct decision.) After fifteen or twenty nervous minutes, those of us from the *Vavilov*, already on shore, are told to get ready. There will have to be two races, if the *Ioffe* runners are able to get in at all.

There is another change. The wind chill factor on the glacier is a real worry. We will have many slow runners (and walkers) including older people. To prevent hypothermia from exposure on the glacier, there will be a double loop to the Chinese base at the other end of the course instead of a second climb up the glacier. Coats and scarves are shed at the last moment before the start. Runners, get set...Go!

The mud is unbelievable. It looks as though somebody has been driving tanks through this stuff – it turns out this is true. The course is on a sort of heavy equipment road between the four bases, and it is well traveled. The overnight cold weather hasn't come close to freezing the mud, either. The better runners are up ahead, but not by much. After a couple of miles the mud gets more manageable. The first stream crossings are easy, with enough gravel islands to hop across. Some of the hills are steep, and nearly everyone walks them. Some are a hundred feet high, others only thirty, but they all slow us. Approaching Artigas we see a beautiful bay on the right, with a glacier ending in sheer ice cliffs. Uruguayans from the base, a group of five or six, are shouting and waving happily. Their base has been cleaned and painted for their President's visit. Out of respect for their effort, we are running behind the base rather than through. My water bottles are nowhere in the box; oh well, onward up the glacier.

The pace slows here as we pick our way through crusty ice with areas obviously melting, up a 750-foot hill. The lack of sun is a blessing here, as are the ridges of fresh snow that provide the best footing. The course is marked with little pink flags on wires stuck into the snow. In the stiff wind, the flags are making tense zipping sounds. After we have climbed for several minutes, the leaders come in sight, returning down the glacier from the turn-around point above us.

I have never before run in a race where I knew the face of every other runner. The community feeling is contagious. Euphoria breaks out as the leaders pass by coming down. Every passing on the glacier is an occasion for encouragement, grins, shouts. We are really here, really doing this thing – each knowing that every other runner has planned for this moment just about as long as we have, and feeling the same elation.

Each runner in turn rounds the flag at the top of the course and heads back down the glacier, this time passing runners coming up and trading more grins and encouragement. Lower on the glacier the footing gets sloppy. This ice is no place for a tumble with twenty miles still to go. The runners are now spread out and the first ten or so are well ahead, with another ten spaced out at hundred-meter intervals behind me. The same hills and streams are crossed as we return to the start. It would be nice to have one more plank on the big stream close to Artigas but with some fancy stepping I am able to keep my feet dry. The last mile down into Bellingshausen is thick mud again. I try running farther up on the high edge of the road but even the un-driven-on mud there is too soft. All right, they warned us, at least the mud is easy on the knees and ankles even if it's hard on the quad muscles. For heaven's sake don't pull a muscle here.

Passing Bellingshausen at ten miles I grab a quick drink of liquid and surrender one place. The Gatorade has been sitting out in the weather. It tastes great but chills the body to the core. The wind continues to rip at the nylon shell I am wearing, and I pull my ski cap down to eye level because it feels like it will blow off.

A stream, deep, fast, and with no bridge, separates the Russian and Chilean bases. One foot has to go into the icy torrent, followed by a great leap over the rest of the channel. The landing is a hard one, into a steep gravel bank. We'll have to jump this thing (and anything else between here and the Chinese base) six times before we are done. A few Chileans are out of doors, mostly working, as we trot up the hill along one of their streets and on out of "town" over a similar road to the first one, but drier and more solid. It's a mile and a half over the hill to the Great Wall station. Skuas hover overhead, looking menacing at first until I recall reading that researchers at Bellingshausen have tamed skuas as pets. Apparently there was an international tempest one year when some of the Chinese caught and ate a skua that the Russians had raised from infancy. In the confining world of Antarctic base life, human society is tenacious about its few luxuries, and the same skua that represented the luxury of pet-keeping also represented the luxury of a good meal.

The road to the Chinese base affords scenic views of green mossy hills and rocky beaches. There is a metal bridge over the last creek (though I have two very wet feet by now), and I follow two other runners up into the base, wondering where the turnaround is and what kind of welcome awaits us there. Last night aboard ship, Thom remarked that the Chinese received him quite coolly this time, despite having been very enthusiastic on the 1995 trip. The world is a different place now.

Not a soul is in sight at the Great Wall base. Furthermore, the little flags that marked the course are nowhere to be seen. Suddenly it dawns on me that the metal footbridge – the one we just crossed below the base – was probably the turnaround point. Kevin and another runner ahead of me are well into the Chinese station. We all turn around and run out, having added half a mile to a mile to what is going to be a long day already. On the way back we warn other runners, but some will repeat the same mistake. It is true that missing turns is part of trail running – but I would like to have that half-mile back.

In the middle miles many are running alone in the cold and the harsh wind, and getting ample time to reflect. The immediate realities are a muddy supply road at the bottom of the world, a carnivorous skua hovering overhead and whitecaps rolling down the harbor. We runners and the scientists at any of these bases may share a desire to scale heights, explore and conquer, but to live here means weeks and months in which mud, ice and skuas are the only realities away from tiny modular rooms, quarters, instruments and the calendar. At the end of this run we will return to our warm ship, and hot shower, and meals that show us we haven't really left the comforts of home and human society after all. For us to run today is a luxury. But the humans who live at these bases are just as dependent on their modules as we are on our ship. We are all adventurers. We fight and flee the things that limit our lives. We run, pushing against distance and gravity, the same as we would anywhere else. And at the end, back where life is warmer and more congenial, both runner and scientist alike will proudly say "I was there!"

We retrace the road over the hill to Chile, splash across the big stream, and pass the multi-directional signpost in Russian that represents the start/finish line ("Molodezhnaya 13100 km"). The race clock that Thom brought all the way from Boston reads 1:42 for half a marathon, and there are smiles all around. Two runners near me are done – they only wanted to do a half-marathon. This means I'll be more alone than ever. I head back out through the mud towards Uruguay, trailing "Bill," a dentist living in Saudi Arabia. I'm a little better now at avoiding the muck and streams. The green mossy hills, white with a dusting of show, are actually looking friendly. It's a quiet three miles out to Artigas and beyond to the base of the glacier where we will turn back instead of climbing the ice a second time. I meet walkers just coming off the glacier for the first time – we really are spread out. This time I also discover my green water bottle in a box at the glacier – I carry it the half-mile back to Artigas and leave it in the box there, from which it will again disappear.

On the return march to Bellingshausen, now power-walking more uphills than before, I am conscious of being hungry. That is a sign of weakening. This is no time to lose energy, we have come too far now. I decide to take a long, frigid drink of Gatorade and hope the calories and electrolytes get me through. But the hunger is working on me. I leap the big stream again, immediately chilling the foot that was warm, and take a wrong turn. There are no runners in sight ahead of me, and the Chilean base, much the most developed of the four bases on our route, has several streets, an airport, a heating system, and occupies a fair amount of land. I find myself going up a hill, which is okay, but it's the wrong hill. Two or three slower runners, still on the right road, are by now past me. I plunge across through the mud between two bright orange buildings and make my way onto the right path. I have lost a few minutes and several places. I know it really doesn't matter but it's disheartening anyway. I am now even hungrier, and there are still six miles to go. Rather than attack the rest of the hill, I choose to power-walk it and calm myself. I won't catch the runners who passed me. I will finish. My time so far is good enough that I will easily beat four hours if I keep my head. I will get something to eat when I pass Bellinsghausen again before the last three miles. From the other direction, here come the winners on their way to the finish – good job! I make it to the top of the hill and then briskly begin to stride down the other side, enjoying the day again. The skuas are still hovering, but I am not about to be skua food today.

After crossing the bridge below the Chinese base, I turn about only to face an older Japanese runner approaching the bridge from the other side. Here is a social dilemma. He bows and tells me to go first. That is clearly against protocol, but I don't have all day. I cross quickly, compliment him on his effort, and head back to where I know the food is.

Nearing Bellingshausen again, heavy fatigue is setting in. I storm across the big stream, shout "one more" as I round the pole – and then veer off the course, up the stairs and into the rec building. A terrific spread of food from the *Vavilov* is on the table in the movie room. I grab a raspberry coffee cake slice, eat it, and run out the door and across the big creek with half a bagel in hand. Few big city marathons have better amenities than that. Now one more trip to China and my Antarctic marathon will be history. The clock says 3:17, plenty of time. Power-walk the hill, taking the correct road through Chile this time, run down the other side. Suddenly both thighs cramp at the same time. That's dehydration and low electrolytes but there isn't anything I can do about it. I jog through the twenty-four-mile mark then out to the bridge below Great Wall for the last turn. A mile and a half left. Another runner, Shalako, is there, offering encouragement. He is on his second trip to the bridge, I on my third. I run crampily back through the creeks and under the skuas, up the hill for the last time, and then power one continuous fast three-quarter mile straight through the big stream and up to the finish. Nobody at the finish line is watching me. They are trying to make a penguin go to the finish line. So I make exaggerated "I'm done" gestures and they check me in at 3:41:45. A pretty good time, considering the mud, hills, mud, detours, streams, mud…and the biting wind that has blown the whole time.

Inside the rec room there is hot soup. I pop the mini-bottle of champagne I bought in Ushuaia and drain it, silently thanking everything that got me here. Then soup and more soup, bagels, empanadas, soup. More than enough for an army. The *Ioffe* runners have arrived and are about an hour into their race. Russians are everywhere around the room, from the ship and from the base. Food from the ships will be left on shore as thanks for hosting us. Outside, the 0°F wind chill is keeping everyone in. Matthew from the *Vavilov* appears at regular intervals to poll for anyone wishing to return to the ship. After a few more eats, I change into dry things and hip boots, and take a last commemorative picture or two on the rocky beach. The wind is still high and the bay is choppy, with whitecaps coming straight at the Zodiacs on the trip back.

The ship is warm and cozy, a floating island of comfort in a land of perpetual discomfort. Hot shower water, warm clothes, hot tea and drinks and everybody is eager to swap stories. The day has been a legend in its own right, at least within the lives of those who ran. Masami from Japan has set a new women's record for the continent! The guy on the *Ioffe*, Scott Dvorak, ran a very fast time, beating Ray Brown and Michael Collins from our ship, though they did not race head-to-head because the two ships' groups started at different times. The awards ceremony and party with the *Ioffe* will be postponed due to rough weather and the day's scrambled logistics. The big diesels purr through the night. There is no sleep like the sleep after a marathon.

Tuesday, February 18   —   Gerlache Strait

Post-race stiff muscles awaken me early, but the coffee is hot and the bridge is open as always. We are in a different world, many miles from King George Island – in fact, from the whole South Shetland chain. The captain has sailed full speed all night with the spotlights on to look for icebergs, and we are now in the Gerlache Strait between the mainland Antarctic Peninsula and a heavily glaciated island.

The first landing this morning is at Neko Harbor, a small inlet on the mainland. We will officially be on the continent here. Our Zodiac group is still well back in the boarding order, which is all right with me for I'm in no mood to hurry this morning. Ashore, we find pink and gray granite rocks, a change from the volcanic sand and soils of the South Shetlands, and here all the penguins are Gentoos rather than the chinstraps that predominated up north. I have to lie prone to get a good panorama shot, but there is no guano on the rocks. Gilles provides information about fault lines in the jagged exposed cliffs. The Gerlache Strait would be a rock climber's paradise in a warmer climate.

A small red wooden building, barely a toolshed, stands high on the rocky beach and contains kerosene and emergency food rations. It has been built by the Norwegians, and the harbor is named after the *Neko*, a Norwegian ship that found shelter here. The inside of the hut is dark and worse than cheerless. This would be a very tough place to try to survive, but with food and fuel and a known location it would probably keep a few individuals alive for some time.

The Zodiacs have had to make a long run through floating bits of ice to reach land at Neko harbor, and the trip back is similarly circuitous and fun. Whales are seen sporadically. Under way again, we pass another vessel whose passengers are on their way to a landing at Couverville Island. A Marine Expeditions staff member tells me that ships in the area keep in radio contact to ensure that no two call at the same landing at the same time, and that they keep out of sight of each other if possible, to avoid spoiling the splendid sense of isolation. We are less alone than we feel, but still very much alone. The *Vavilov* passes through dramatic scenery all afternoon, heading for the spectacular Lemaire Passage. The sky is clearing and afternoon sunlight is slanting across the water onto the peaks and ridges of the mainland. All passengers, and most hands, come out on deck as the Russian helmsman begins to thread the narrow channel, slowly dodging ice bits and larger bergs while we gape at the vertical walls of rock on either side. It is a masterful demonstration of agility in steering a ship, amid an even more masterful demonstration of natural beauty. Arriving at the far end, we once more hop into the Zodiacs and land at Pleneau Island with the sun already low in the sky.

We have reached 65°7' south. The long twilight is gathering, all are tired from yesterday's run, the scenery, the time outside. It is still around 35°F but feels colder. The island is mainly large granite rock surfaces that look ice-scoured. Adelie penguins, with spectacle-like circles around each eye, are present here. The majority are Gentoos, but some of these still have chicks in the nest. This surprises the naturalist Robin, who says they should be at sea by now. The strait to the west is choked with bergs of the most fantastic shapes and grotesque aspect. This makes for exciting photos. The heavy clouds of the past few days are long gone, and the lighter streaks of white that remain in the sky augment the forms of icebergs and rocky peaks. Late afternoon light from the west holds every aspect of the landscape in a sense of peace and calm. Many in the group are affected, as each simply finds a quiet spot and chooses to stand alone in the beauty.

And so the summer evening lengthens. The tide moves slowly, carrying drift ice with it while motionless peaks regard the broad twilight bowl of sky. Time is always too short, whether it is measured in moments like this, or in the years of a penguin or the millennia of a mountain or the millions of years of continental drift. Eventually each human in our company is carried back by a Zodiac to the only environment in which we can actually live. The ship turns north. I am alone on deck as we navigate the Lemaire Passage again. The peaks are in shadow but the light is lingering, as it does for hours here every evening. Amazingly, there are almost no icebergs in the passage this time. They have moved with the speed of the currents and tides.

Below, there is much talk of the seven continents, and not just in terms of marathons. Marathon Tours has promoted the "seven continents" theme in connection with this race; however, the idea was first mentioned to me thirteen years ago. By my wife, in our Tokyo kitchen after eight years of cultural acclimatization culminating in a decision to leave Japan and move to Australia. I love to remind her of this whenever my urge to travel and run seems obsessive.

Other modes of adventure get discussed as well. An Australian muses that he'd love to try climbing "the seven summits," meaning the highest point on each of the seven continents. Then the group discovers that he hasn't even walked to the highest point in his own country, Mt. Kosciusko, little more than a day hike with a sack lunch. There are hoots of laughter all around. There are already mountaineers in the world who have done all seven, and access to the more difficult ones, Everest, Denali, and particularly

Vinson in Antarctica, is becoming easier every year as the search for peak adventure experiences becomes an industry.

Two teachers from Washington, D.C., are more practical adventurers. They have brought donated digital cameras and satellite uplink equipment and can often be found in the ship's library uploading their photos immediately after a landing, keeping them in touch with their students daily. This high-tech approach may become normal some day, but in early 1997 it feels like the leading edge.

We have only one more day here in maritime Antarctica. Early in the night, the *Vavilov* anchors in a sheltered location at Paradise Bay and shuts off its engines. Accustomed by now to motion and diesel vibrations, I sleep fitfully in the stillness and rise before 6:00 a.m.

WEDNESDAY, FEBRUARY 19 ⚊ PARADISE BAY

The first order today is landing at Bahia Paraiso (Paradise Bay), an Argentine base. Half of the ship tours the bay by Zodiac while the other half slides down the slope behind Almirante Brown Station. I elect to stand around, helping three young Argentines sled an oil drum over the main building from their quarters. They move at glacial speed, clearly bored with the routine. The base is being rebuilt after a fire 25 years ago started by a mad captain who wanted to be relieved of his post. Today it is difficult to see why he felt that way – the bay is spectacular.

I head off on my own to a vantage point behind a building and play nature photographer, shooting frame after frame of a pair of sheathbills who are harassing a feeding penguin. The young penguin taps the side of the beak of its parent, an action that starts a regurgitation reflex in the parent and also invites an attack from the sheathbills that skillfully steal the regurgitated krill and ferry it back to their own scruffy chick waiting unguarded beside the foundation. They have chosen only this one penguin parent to harass, even though several others are feeding nearby.

It must appear vulnerable somehow. I don't know why nobody picks on the sheathbill chick. There are few skuas here.

Three humpback whales swim around the near part of the bay, their blowing audible in the absence of engine noise. Lazily they pass between the ship and shore, then move out towards open water.

I have done well not to join the sledding party on the hill. One passenger is injured and is taken to the ship on the Argentines' Zodiac. When our turn comes for the Zodiac tour of the bay the luck gets even better. A white crabeater seal on an ice floe yawns and poses for the cameras, barely eight feet away. Cormorants wheel and dive all around us, feeding, their loon-like cries ringing around the still bay. Pieces of a blue glacier suddenly calve a few hundred yards away, sending a two-foot wall of waves at the Zodiac. The pilot turns towards the waves and we ride over the swell. The day is magic.

The Argentines have a small store with pins, patches and postcards for the tourist trade. This bay of paradise is bound to be visited by many in future years. May they tread lightly and take only photographs as we have done. The maps show the base buildings where we stand as being on an island in the bay, however it does not appear that way to the eye. The glacier pushing off the continent reaches the island today; some future year may see it recede and leave open water behind the base as well as in front. Even in paradise, there is change.

No organized race is complete without an award ceremony. The *Ioffe* arrives in the bay by early afternoon and sends its passengers by Zodiac over to the *Vavilov* for a barbecue on the aft deck. It is like a first meeting with unknown relatives. Their ship is identical to ours, right down to the artificial flowers in the vases in the dining rooms. They have sailed some of the same waters and made some of the same landings that we made. Our experiences with the marathon were not identical, however. We learn that they stood on deck watching through binoculars as our race started. Arriving after the *Vavilov* they had a more distant, less favorable anchorage and were unable to get a Zodiac safely to shore through the rough waves. After a couple of hours their steward announced that the midday meal would be served, and being unlikely to land they were advised to go ahead and eat hearty. Immediately after lunch, however, it was determined that the waves had abated and landing could proceed. So the *Ioffe* runners were grateful for the break in the weather that allowed them to run the marathon they had trained for, but many had run on a full stomach, not advisable under any conditions. After two or three hours the visitors depart, we raise anchor and move northward.

On the *Vavilov* we have been lucky. Despite the gray weather at Half Moon and Aitcho our tour and race have run on schedule, and we are able to count twelve landings including Paradise Bay this morning.

And the last landing of the trip is the finest. Couverville Island looked like a nondescript penguin colony when we first passed it on Tuesday. My landing group has worked itself around to being first again and as we board the Zodiac for the trip in, a small minke whale in the channel sights us. Instead of landing we head over for a look. The whale has the same thought. It is as curious about the Zodiac as we are about it, nosing about and diving under, and coming close enough to touch our black rubber pontoons. Suddenly there is a whale at my elbow, near enough to touch, its eye less than a yard from mine. In that instant I realize I could touch the animal, and also realize that I will not do so. Let it be, and may all life in this land continue to live as untouched as possible. Much film is used in a matter of minutes and thirty lucky humans in the first three Zodiacs are left speechless by the encounter with this wild giant of the Antarctic oceans.

The landing represents a farewell. Having grown fond of these surroundings, many of the runners on the *Vavilov* focus on what they like best, penguin-watching, picture-taking, hiking, or simply gazing. All around are wave-polished stones, so easy to slip into one's pockets and then onto one's mantelpiece at home. Some in our party may do this, and my own predilection for bringing stones home is well established. The encounters with the minke whale, the mosses of Aitcho, the penguins of Bailey Head, and the solemn promises of the Antarctic tourist win out, however. I am proud to say that I did not pick up a souvenir rock. My rock is still there on its patch of exposed beach. Ishmael came home with only a story, and it was enough.

I photograph penguins sliding down an ice ramp on their way to the water, then find tufts of Antarctic grass, and a large boulder with green-white serpentine intrusions. I am full of questions and seek out a staff scientist. After a lesson on magmatic intrusions and Antarctic plants by Gilles, I am on the last Zodiac out – and lucky again, this time cruising within fifty yards of a pair of humpbacks in the channel. The sound of the approaching Zodiac is too much for the whales, who dive beneath me – a brief underwater glance at a white face with its tiny eye – and are gone. The mood on board is euphoric.

Dinner is lavish and again eaten heartily, which is probably a mistake. Within three hours we exit the sheltered waters off the Antarctic Peninsula and are back in the Drake Passage, which is considerably less quiet than last time. I try Bonine, which gives me a splitting headache, which I then try to cover with Tylenol.

THURSDAY, FEBRUARY 20 ━ AT SEA

Most of this day is spent sleeping. Despite the action of the stabilizers the *Vavilov* is pitching and rolling on large swells. It may be a normal day on the Drake Passage, but walking about is not much fun. Add the sedative effects of seasickness remedies and fatigue from a week of excitement, and the result is a day happily spent dozing. There is time for the occasional trip on deck but the appearance of a solitary albatross is not as exciting as it was a week ago. A tour of the ship's inner workings is offered for those who feel up to it, but they will have to write that story themselves. I take another nap, then wake briefly for dinner and a late watch on the bridge.

Here and there around the ship runners talk of what they will do next, would like to do, consider worth doing. All agree that the whale encounters on Wednesday were wonderful but I realize that many of the high points for me were simply private moments that will always be difficult to share. Each has sought adventure on our own and whatever we may have to say to others, the experiences have affected us in our own private worlds accordingly. The voyage to Antarctica represented a supreme act of escape and challenge to most of us, yet we were never in peril. My adventure was my own, and it is the same for everyone else. I became intensely preoccupied with penguin behavior at Bailey Head, the voyage in and out of Neptune's Bellows, the photographic possibilities of Neko Harbor, Pleneau Island, and Paradise Bay, the serpentine boulders at Couverville. Many others took only a casual interest in these things, and for them the story lies elsewhere. Two in our party will remember this as a wedding cruise.

That the trip has meant something different to each has kept us somewhat separate even during the most euphoric days of the trip. Now that we are returning northward we are pulling into our own personal shells a little more. The end is not yet in sight but it will arrive, and each of us will head to our next adventure. I already know what mine will be; the person who first suggested seven continents to me is supposed to be boarding a plane in Oregon at this moment. We have been out of phone contact for ten days, yet if all goes well we will meet at the hotel in Buenos Aires.

FRIDAY, FEBRUARY 21 — CAPE HORN

A last morning at sea. Lectures on mining economics (Gilles), and ice sheet cores (Stan). Cape Horn is sighted around 2:45 in the afternoon. No continental cape but a craggy island at the end of a chain of rocks and fjords, its appearance has struck terror into the hearts of sailors for centuries. To a ship returning from our direction, however, it looks pretty good. Sun breaks through, and once again all are out on deck to watch. I try to photograph the lighthouse for my youngest child, who this year is a student of lighthouses, but it's two miles away and I'm on a pitching deck. In the evening we settle up ship's accounts and prepare to debark on the morrow. The teachers are showing digital pictures on their laptop. Mine are hidden on film, twenty-seven rolls, and like others I am silently hoping that they are good, perhaps great.

This evening's meal is the Captain's Dinner, and Captain Beluga compliments us on a good race and a great voyage. This gracious, well-educated man has skillfully taken us across the Drake Passage twice, performed a marriage, run the ship all night after the marathon to get us out of the weather and into good sightseeing, and all the time allowed anyone to come onto the bridge at any time of day or night. He lets us know that the exciting trip southbound through the ice in the Lemaire Passage was steered by his third mate, who had never done that before. With good humor the Captain chides us for letting a runner from the *Ioffe* win the race, and hopes to see us all again. We all contribute to hearty applause and to tips for the crew. They too have looked after us and will sincerely appreciate some hard currency to spend, which they will divide up in equal shares, from the captain to the youngest engine operator. It's the way they have been brought up.

Saturday, February 22 ⚓ Ushuaia

A group picture is taken on the pier next to the ship. Passengers and crew alike disperse into town according to our individual schedules. I have two and a half hours to get to the airport, which is about two miles away, and welcome the chance to stretch my legs by walking. The peaks on either side of the Beagle Passage look much friendlier now than ten days ago, and the sight of trees on the lower slopes is positively rich. Two of the Russian mates emerge from a shop with a new tape player, probably bought with dollars from our tips. The gift shops in Ushuaia style themselves *Fin del Mundo*, the end of the earth, but Ushuaia is only the end of the road. We have gone to the White Continent, made thirteen landings by Zodiac, and run a marathon. None of these facts really scratches the surface of what one feels when faced with the immenseness of that utterly remote, cold, windy, icy place. The polar world merely begins with what we have seen.

In a matter of weeks the Antarctic shelf ice will begin forming in earnest. Day and night are already nearly equal in length; it is late in the southern summer. Birds will leave the continent, as will nearly all marine mammals. The penguin chicks we saw at Pleneau Island will be too young to survive. Mercy may be a trait of humans, but it is not part of the plan down there. A few of our species will again volunteer to winter over on the White Continent, driven by curiosity or a more powerful desire for escape than I could muster. Others of my species are delivering artificial limbs to landmine victims in Asia.

My feet eventually reach the old air terminal. The aircraft is there and bears us north to warmer lands. After dark, standing at the hotel entrance, I see a familiar figure step off the airport shuttle. It is our twenty-fifth anniversary, the summer night is warm and Buenos Aires is perfect for strolling. There is the presidential palace where Eva Peron lived, here is the waterfront. A historic sailing ship, the *Sarmiento*, is tied up at the wharf, and we can go aboard. The galley still smells of food, the wooden rails and ropes have the touch of decades of sailors' hands. Ships no larger than this carried Melville to the whaling grounds, Shackleton to the Antarctic pack ice. Those were adventures.

Midnight comes and goes, and hundreds of Argentines are still out walking on the riverfront. For my wife of twenty-five years and me, there is a restaurant, a good dry red wine, a breath of the warm summer air. And many stories to tell.

BOOK BAG

David G. Campbell, *The Crystal Desert: Summers in Antarctica*

British Antarctic Survey topographic maps of King George Island, Deception Island, and areas of the western Antarctic Peninsula

Caroline Alexander, *The Endurance: Shackleton's Legendary Antarctic Expedition* or

Alfred Lansing, *Endurance: Shackleton's Incredible Voyage*

The photographs of Frank Hurley, photographer on the *Endurance* expedition

Herman Melville, *Moby Dick, or The Whale*

Africa

A view of Cape Town and Table Mountain from Robben Island, where many political prisoners were held, including Nelson Mandela for seventeen years.

Two Oceans Ultra Marathon
Cape Town, April 1999

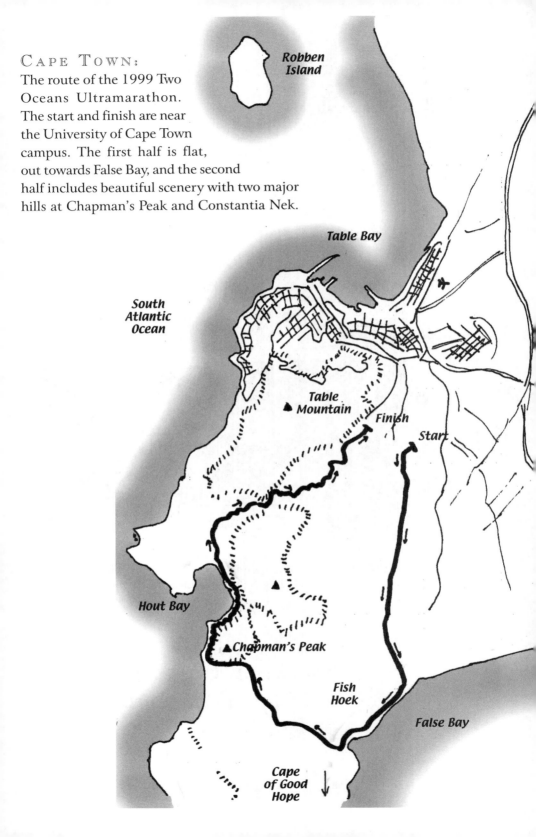

CAPE TOWN:
The route of the 1999 Two
Oceans Ultramarathon.
The start and finish are near
the University of Cape Town
campus. The first half is flat,
out towards False Bay, and the second
half includes beautiful scenery with two major
hills at Chapman's Peak and Constantia Nek.

Robben
Island

Table Bay

South
Atlantic
Ocean

Table
Mountain

Finish

Start

Hout Bay

▲Chapman's Peak

Fish
Hoek

False Bay

Cape
of Good
Hope

CHAPTER 5

When Oceans Meet

Two Oceans Ultramarathon, Cape Town,
South Africa, Easter Weekend, 1999

> *"I was tall and lanky, which Locke said was the ideal*
> *build for a long-distance runner. With a few hints from*
> *him, I began training. I enjoyed the discipline and*
> *solitariness of long-distance running, which allowed me*
> *to escape from the hurly-burly of school life....*
>
> *Running taught me valuable lessons. In cross-coun-*
> *try competition, training counted more than innate*
> *ability, and I could compensate for a lack of natural*
> *aptitude with diligence and discipline. I applied this in*
> *everything I did. Even as a student, I saw many young*
> *men who had great natural ability but who did not*
> *have the self-discipline and patience to build on their*
> *endowment."*
>
> Nelson Mandela, *Long Walk to Freedom*

I

Oceans meet off southern Africa. A mile or more beneath the
surface, cold, heavy Atlantic waters move southwards in abys-

sal darkness, slowly joining the perpetual flow eastward around Antarctica. Some of this water enters the deepest level of the Indian Ocean basin, some flows on to Chile, diverts northward into the Pacific basin, and circulates there in vast gyres. Deep Pacific waters rise to the surface, becoming warmer, and eventually flow back westward through the East Indies and around the Indian subcontinent. The same water that passes here today in the deep may return decades later as the warm surface current flowing in the other direction around the cape. The Cape of Good Hope. Named by a Portuguese king because it raised the promise of a route to the east. It may be that the true dividing line between the oceans is at Cape Agulhas, the southernmost point in Africa, but in history and in the popular imagination it is the dramatic rocky promontory of the Cape of Good Hope that symbolizes the meeting of these two oceans.

Here there is no separation between Indian and Atlantic, back-fence neighbors without so much as a back fence, only a broad expanse of back yard in which each lives barely a skin apart from the other. There are minor physical differences. One is warmer, saltier, and the other cooler, clearer, and less saline. Cultural differences. One is named after a lost continent fabled in Western mythology and faces sea lanes to Europe and the Americas. The other is also named after a land, in distant geological times a continent also, that instead of sinking and becoming lost moved northward, bumped into Asia and became a subcontinent with the highest mountains on earth. At the southern tip of Africa neither of the oceans nor any of the currents, nor the cape, bears a name that is African in origin.

The first steps around the corner of the continent from the west were easy and inviting. In 1488 Bartholomeus Dias rounded the cape, a difficult accomplishment in the strong surface currents and winds from the east at this latitude. With the use of sail designs borrowed from dhows of the Indian Ocean, the Portuguese mariner was able to sail closer to the wind than other European seafarers, and thereby eastward into his neighbor's side of the back yard. Within a generation caravels and carracks were every-where opening new routes from the Atlantic to the East. Kilwa was sacked by Portuguese in the early 1500s, and one by one other Swahili trade centers were destroyed or occupied. The Atlantic prospered as never before. The losers were the inland trade routes collectively known as the Silk Road, which cut through the heart of the Islamic world and had fueled the prosperity of its golden era from the eighth through the fifteenth century.

For five hundred years after Columbus, the treasures of southern Africa and beyond were bought, bartered for, or simply acquired by Atlantic peoples. The land at the meeting of the two oceans was occupied and claimed by Boers and British, Germans and Portuguese, even as the Zulu people were becoming a nation within.

British, Boers and Zulus all fought each other and it wasn't as lopsided as some colonial battles. Boer and British guns were pitted against the Zulu *assegai*, a short stabbing spear, and Zulu close-rank formation fighting that in some ways resembles the field tactics of the Athenians at the Battle of Marathon.

Tensions between the European rivals pushed the Boers inland to the Orange Free State and Transvaal while Britain occupied the Cape in 1806 and then obtained the large Cape Province by treaty in 1814. This led to a notion that, as F.W. DeKlerk put it much later, (South) Africa could be like a little Europe with many little nations each founded for its own people. Sep-arateness. In Afrikaans, *apartheid*. This would eventually mean forcing black Africans into separate districts for living even as the industrial and extraction economy was forcing many to seek work in white territory.

By the later twentieth century the world at last found African separateness repugnant. International isolation and mounting internal pressures led to the end of apartheid and the release of Nelson Mandela in 1992. Once again the Eastern, Western, and African-origin people of Africa were in the same yard with few fences, one ocean without borders. Neighbors, although with differences old and new.

By 1994 Nelson Mandela was elected to a five-year term as President of South Africa. By early 1999 he was preparing to step down and new elections were afoot. The last months of his presidency seemed like an excellent time to visit the New South Africa and run one of the classic road races of the African continent, the Two Oceans.

II

Redeye flight to Miami, another overnight flight fourteen hours to Cape Town, arriving mid-afternoon. It is Easter Week. I've been watching the weather reports, lows of 70 and highs of 82 or so, but somehow it is 93°F when we climb off the plane. Grass-fire smoke burns the throat.

The airport is small and basic, with signs in English, Afrikaans and something else that might be Xhosa, about claiming the correct bag and "building Africa together." The bus into town passes mile after mile of corrugated metal squatter shacks, then heads downtown and to the Waterfront, with a spectacular view of Table Mountain above a well-protected harbor.

At the hotel, the group meets formally. My roommate has climbed Everest! Much talk of "what have you run, and where..." ensues, stories topping other stories. "Do you know so-and-so who ran the Nepal Stage Race last year?" A couple of runners lace up their shoes and head out. I elect to remain idle, given the heat and travel fatigue.

Over the next two days, we are taken to the Table Mountain tramway for an eagle's eye view of the city and bay, and a walk around the flat mountain top features a number of species of *fynbos*, native only to the Cape area and rarest of the six major branches of the plant kingdom.

One afternoon a few runners join me on the hydrofoil ferry out to Robben Island, the prison camp in the bay where political prisoners were held in the days of apartheid. Nelson Mandela spent seventeen of his twenty-seven years of imprisonment here. Our guide, Elias Mzamo, was himself a former political prisoner in the same cells we are visiting. The tour would be unforgettable in any event but Mr. Mzamo makes it come alive. With quiet dignity he describes not only beatings and forced labor but also the in-camp "university" system. In this each-one-teach-one arrangement among the prisoners, those who were highly educated acted as instructors to the others. There were even examinations written by candlelight and concealed from the guards by cleverly folded blankets, done on the same weeks that universities on the mainland were holding their own exams. Mr. Mzamo describes himself without irony as "a graduate of the University of F Block," the building where the political prisoners were kept.

On the day before the race, we are given a tour of the Cape area by bus. We drive southward along False Bay on the east side of the cape, past beaches and areas of one-story houses. These will be the early miles of the race tomorrow, flat and fast, during and after sunrise. At Fish Hoek we stop for lunch and watch the people around us, nearly all white. A black security guard stands at the entrance to a car park, in uniform. A very young white mother in a two-piece swim suit is curled up with her infant in the sun on the beach near the boardwalk. Both are asleep in the intense noontime sun. The baby is uncovered and getting a sunburn.

III

Take a large fish tank, divided into four parts by boards. Fill each of the four parts with a water of a different temperature, or salinity, or mineral content, but most importantly of a different color. Now take some of the water from one part out and put it in another tank.

This is the basic shape of the widely accepted "out of Africa" theory of human evolution. The four races of Africa are still in

Africa today, the majority Bantu population, the tall, slim Nilotic people of the upper Nile, the smallest people on earth, often called Pygmies, and the small, light brown Xhoisan or Bushmen. Based on the timetables of genetic change, the theory finds that all the other people of the world are descended from a group that left Africa in distant prehistory.

Once this group was "out of Africa" they spread and migrated and populated the rest of the planet. This a thought worth considering at some length. This means that *all* groups of everyone "else," including Australian aboriginals, blue-eyed Norwegians, Arabs, Japanese, even the people of the upper Amazon, are more closely related than any of the four African groups are to each other.

Going along with the "out of Africa" theory, suppose that some of the water you removed from one part of the tank became the Arabic culture, and some became Indian, and some became European. In time, each of these found its way back onto the African continent. Put some of the water back into the other three parts of the tank, but don't mix it yet. Just place it there.

Now remove the boards that divide the four parts of the fish tank. For a time, nothing will appear to happen except that the waters will diffuse slightly into each other so that the boundaries are less visible. Density differences may cause some water to slide across below or above other water. Suppose we rotate the tank, or better yet suppose that something, like a fish, swims from one part of the tank into another. The result is turbulence.

Bodies of water sliding past each other first make large whorls and counterflows, then smaller eddies on either side where one or the other color is more concentrated for a while. The same happens with history. The earliest cultural records in Southern Africa are Xhoisan. The Bantu migrations reached the area centuries ago. European outposts appeared on the coast early in the colonial period. Then at a time just before the European culture began to spread inland, there occurred a major event in southern African history called the *mfecane* or "crushing," characterized by the appearance and growth of the Zulu nation and the larger-than-life person of Shaka Zulu.

The out-of-wedlock son of a socially disadvantaged mother, Shaka grew up as a loner, teased by other Zulu youth. An imposing physical specimen, he became a devoted student of combat, refining traditional techniques and inventing new ones. In time he defeated rivals and became a military leader, then a chief. Once Shaka was chief, boys were separated from their parents and raised communally so that nobody would have an advantage based on parentage. Forbidden to court or marry for reasons of discipline, boys grew into warriors whose personal loyalties were primarily to their peers.

Zulu warriors under Shaka were trained to run barefoot over thorns, lest the loss of a sandal make them easy prey in a battle. They learned to grapple with an enemy and kill with a short spear thrust to the side. Battlefield tactics emphasized close ranks and reinforcement of positions so as to overcome numerical disadvantages. Above all they were disciplined. Disobedience, loss of weapons or nerve in battle, or insubordination could be punished by immediate death at spearpoint.

The Zulu people numbered only a few thousand when Shaka was born, but grew to considerable numbers by assimilating surrounding tribes. A vanquished opponent, given the option to become Zulu or die, usually became Zulu. Rather than face warriors they could not defeat, many other neighboring populations abandoned their farm and pasture lands and fled, sometimes over considerable distances, to avoid the Zulu military juggernaut.

Shaka is interpreted variously as a brilliant symbol of African power, a despot, a warrior genius, a Napoleon. It is clear that by the time of his assassination in 1828 his fighters, possible the best hand-to-hand fighters in history, had met their match in the European rifle, and also that his skills as a civil administrator were hard up against the demands of the European colonizing force. Still the legends of Shaka and of Zulu strength remain powerful. One wonders what might have happened if the technological advantages of the Europeans had not been so overwhelming in the early 1800s.

Suppose: On a key travel route in Natal, a standoff between Zulu and British forces. A Zulu phalanx is formed with an intentionally weak center, and charges the British who are temporarily without their cavalry. The British commander assumes that his forces are superior and orders a countercharge on foot against the Zulu center only to find that the flanks close in on him in superior numbers, assegais at the ready, The British panic and flee to a marshy area, where they are done in to the last man. A lone Zulu in full battle array immediately cleans the blood from his blade as required by custom and runs twenty-four miles to the capital of the Zulu people spreading word of the victory. Knowing that the other British forces in the region will fall on the capital, the full Zulu army follows as fast as they can, being trained to run barefoot for additional speed. On arrival, the Zulus man the battlements and shout defiance at the British forces closing in on the capital. Seeing that they are at a disadvantage and not wanting to incur two disasters in one day, the British retreat, abandon their plans to colonize and withdraw to Gibraltar and Suez.

It's the story of the Battle of Marathon, obviously, told from the standpoint of a local people repelling the foreign invader. Athens fought off the invading forces of Persia, but Athenian-style democracy was hardly a characteristic of Zulu society. It might be more accurate to say that Zulu life in the time of Shaka was more Spartan than Sparta, but above all it was African.

Well, Marathon didn't happen in southern Africa, for dozens of reasons. It's even more difficult to imagine a second Battle of Salamis, with small maneuverable African ships ramming and sinking larger invading craft in the shallow waters, say between Cape Town and Robben Island. The British had a considerable advantage in communications and technology, already had multiple footholds on the continent, and most importantly had the ability to stand back and shoot rifles at an enemy whose superior hand-to-hand skills were rendered all but useless. For the next

180 years the region would be administered, first colonially and then as a federation, by British and Afrikaner.

I am not a professional historian, and I cannot compete with the experts any more than I can run in the lead pack in a marathon. But even I can see that by the time the Afrikaners trekked inland to carve out territory in the Orange Free State and the Transvaal, and the British had established the Cape colony, most of the African groups in the area had been doubly displaced, once by the Zulu and once again by the European colonists. Add to this 150 or so years of colonial government combined with the imposition of *apartheid*, and by the late twentieth century the black peoples of South Africa were a long way indeed from their traditional lands and livelihoods prior to the *mfecane*. The partitions in society were firmly in place. The mixing of colors became difficult and then was made illegal.

South Africa would eventually see leaders of heroic stature who would make tremendous strides towards righting the imbalance. This is the birthplace, not only of Mandela and Desmond Tutu, but also of Gandhi.

When Nelson Mandela was released in 1992, and the laws of *apartheid* were stricken from the books, it was as if partitions in the waters had suddenly been removed again. Only this time, the economic realities were far different. Transportation by rail and air was available, and migration to the cities for jobs was long an accepted reality, introducing mixing among African groups that had previously lived apart. In the 1994 elections, the Zulu Freedom Party *Inkatha* openly evoked the powerful but also threatening legacy of Shaka.

By the time of my arrival in 1999, only a few years after the removal of the partitions, the signs of open mixing are evident, but certainly the signs of separation predominate.

IV

The bus tour continues. Political posters are on nearly every utility pole, black, yellow and green for the ruling African National Congress (ANC). In some of the other towns down the cape, opposition party posters are dominant. After lunch, still following the Two Oceans Ultramarathon Course, the bus crosses a flat rural area over to the Atlantic side and begins to climb a road cut into the side of a mountain. The first climb is called Little Chapman's Peak, a steady rise over two or three kilometers followed by a moderate downhill. Then the winding climb begins in earnest, a couple of kilometers long and seven hundred feet up on Chapman's Peak road, with a dizzying and spectacular view to the left over Hout Bay and the Atlantic beyond. The road does not go to the top of the mountain, fortunately, but coming between 32 and 35 kilometers (mile 20 and 22) on the course this climb is in a tough spot. It's analogous to Heartbreak Hill in Boston, but higher and steeper. Then once you hit the twenty-six-mile marathon mark in this race, nine more miles remain, including another 700-foot climb to a pass in the rocky hills known as Constantia Nek. And after that, still ten rolling kilometers to the finish. Fifty-six kilometers of road in all. Thirty-five miles.

The bus pauses in Hout Bay to give us a chance to stretch our legs, walk, and bargain for souvenirs. Here as in so many places vendors sit with a gallimaufry of carvings, glassware, shirts, or other wares spread out on blankets. The most noticeable items are the tall giraffes, anywhere from a foot or so up to eight or ten feet or more. The taller the giraffe you give someone as a present, it is said, the greater your respect for that person. My respect for those back home will be limited to the length of my duffel bag.

We prevail on the driver to take a short detour to Constantia Nek for a look at our second major hill. The highway is winding and shaded, and the hill is long. It is a full three kilometers up, and as we take the curves, imagining how we will feel on this grade tomorrow, we suddenly see an actual runner on the road, straining up the hill alongside the bus. Then another runner ahead of him. Are we hallucinating? Both runners are actually wearing race numbers. Did we miss the day of the race, or did someone place these runners here just to set the scene? Each runner is paced by a bicyclist. Our bus stops at the top of the hill and behold, runners are cresting the hill and going on down the race course as we watch. Our driver dispels the mystery. Today is Friday, and the Two Oceans is in fact on Saturday so we have not missed the start. This is a special run for those who cannot race on Saturday due to religious or other reasons, such as observant Jews, Seventh-day Adventists, and so on. The race committee assigns bicycle pacers for safety, and otherwise uses the Friday run as a dress rehearsal for the real thing. All persons are to be accommodated regardless of creed or custom, and today's times are official. This really is the new South Africa!

We return down Constantia Nek against the flow of the Friday race and see that in fact there are not many runners and most are running alone except for their bicyclists. But thirty miles into the race they are running this hill, not walking it, obviously in excellent shape. What would happen if one of these Friday runners actually won the race? Don't worry, says the driver, that won't happen. Some very, very good runners will be going in the main race on Saturday.

Dinner Friday night is pasta on the waterfront, delicious and eminently affordable. Parties of runners are dining everywhere around us, dispelling pre-race nerves by talking expansively and enjoying life. To the south, a peculiar sight; a sheet of cloud is spilling over the top of Table Mountain toward the city as if from a carton of dry ice, tumbling down the slope towards us and vanishing into thin air on the lower slopes. This is the "table cloth" phenomenon, and my guide book says that it is a harbinger of rain or cold weather. This is excellent news because it has been hot since we got here, and with thirty-five miles to run tomorrow every degree is going to count. I go to bed early, set the alarm for 4:00 a.m., and think positive thoughts.

V

Race morning. Long before sunrise, bad news. The anticipated cold weather has not arrived, the sky is clear and the predawn air is light and summery. Then the transfer van doesn't show up and all eight of us all pile into one taxi. A crowd is already forming in the street where the race will start. We find places to sit on the grass or on street curbs, and wait, as runners arrive out of the darkness from all directions. Many wear team singlets. Bloemfontein, Pretoria AC, Zimbabwe HAC, Kruger NP Mara Club, with a single letter sewn on the back of the shirt at the top, S for senior, V for veteran, M for master. This denotes the runner's age group, useful in club races which are scored like meets for each age because it lets the runner behind know whether it is worth trying to pass. Today, our Two Oceans race numbers are also worn on both front and back. We are seeded into corrals, A through F. My paper bib has a C corral label as well as a bright yellow sticker that says "International." This gets me a lot of inquiries and encouragement. Here and there others have labels that say "Rest of Africa," and some of these wear singlets from places like Harare or Gaborone. Those going for their tenth, fifteenth, twentieth Two Oceans finish have special bib colors. Those who have finished over ten Two Oceans are given their own permanent entry numbers, which strikes me as a wonderful idea.

Twenty minutes before the start, the road is filled with runners from curb to curb. The temperature is at least 70°F and the sun has not yet risen. A crescendo of excited chatter in English and Afrikaans. Most of the runners in my corral are white-skinned, but with a good many Asian-looking individuals and some who are darker. One young guy next to me tells a few onlookers that he is running this race as a warmup for a 50-mile ultramarathon he's going to do in his home town of Johannesburg. Someone asks when that race is. "Tomorrow," he says. "I'm flying back this afternoon."

Five minutes to go. The streamers that separate the corrals go down, and the runners move forward towards the line. We are well back from the start, and will have to give up a few seconds, maybe minutes, until the pack gets going. It is a thirty-five-mile race, however, the longest race of my life, so this is not an issue. The big questions are going to be how hot it gets, how I feel after Chapman's Peak, how I handle the big hill at Constantia Nek, and whether I have anything at all left for the last ten kilometers. Really it will all be about the heat, because the rest will depend on that. There is a time goal, actually, if I want to concern my-self with it. The top ten finishers get gold medals – I won't be among them for sure. But everyone who finishes under 5:30 gets a silver medal, everyone under 6:00 a bronze. If I am able to get to the marathon mark in around four hours, that will leave 90 minutes to go the last nine miles if I want to earn a silver. This is ambitious because those last miles include Constantia Nek and I am not a strong performer up hills. Still it's nice to have 5:30 in mind and if everything goes very well I might be within striking distance in the final miles. On the other hand, a bronze medal for beating six hours seems feasible and would be nice. They will close the finish line at six and a half hours after the start. That would be over eleven minutes per mile. If I am going that slow I probably have no business trying to finish at all, so I hope closing time will not be an issue for me.

The gun goes off at 6:00, and nine thousand runners surge along the road heading south, lined here and there with shops, apartments, light industry. The early miles are run in a crowd, slowly, conserving energy. Here and there a vacant lot appears, and well-hydrated runners scoot into the shadows by the dozens to urinate, then edge back into the pack and continue. The sky begins to lighten and colors appear. Portable toilets stand here and there but the flow of runners is so thick that only a few can actually use them. More are relieving themselves behind the toilets than in them. As the dawn breaks, we come down a long gradual hill and into sight of the beaches of False Bay with their brightly colored rows of changing rooms. A long day of running is under way.

VI

South Africa has a rich running history of major races and champions. The Two Oceans was first run in 1970, but the Comrades, a world-famous eighty-nine-kilometer road race between Durban and Pietermaritzburg, has been run since 1921 except for the years of World War II. The site "safrica.info" is a good source of basic information about the country's greatest runners. One such is Mathews Motshwareteu, whose name means "watch him, he will fall" in his native Sotho. His running style may have been unorthodox, but in the first year after the South African Amateur Athletics Union accepted black athletes, 1978, Motshwareteu dueled and defeated Ewald Bonzet, the dominant white runner and record holder at five and ten thousand meters. He then went on to El Paso, Texas, where he led the UTEP team to multiple NCAA cross-country titles, and won the individual title himself in the process.

Zola Budd first attracted attention as a barefoot teenage runner in local races, then went on to European championships and world records at three and five thousand meters. In between, however, she is best remembered for her decision to circumvent the international boycott on South African athletics by applying for British citizenship on the grounds of her grandfather's nationality. Running for Great Britain in the 1984 Olympics she was involved in an unfortunate collision that knocked the favored Mary Decker-Slaney of the U.S. out of the 3,000 meters. Budd, who might well have won a medal also, finished seventh but was criticized heavily.

Josiah Thugwane burst onto the international scene with a victory in the 1996 Olympic Marathon in Atlanta, followed by a victory at Fukuoka in 2:07 and several other top finishes. Gerd Thys, who also ran for South Africa in Atlanta, has run 2:06:32

in Tokyo and placed third in Boston, only 18 seconds out of first. Frith VandeMerwe holds the women's record in the thirty-five-mile Two Oceans at 3:30:36 and is the first woman to break six hours in the Comrades. Angeline Sephooa of Lesotho has won the Two Oceans in 1997 and 1998 and is back running again, very far ahead of me, in 1999.

The list of champions is only the tip of the iceberg in South African society, where sport of one kind or another plays a major role in many lives. Most South Africans are aware that Nelson Mandela ran as a schoolboy, and he writes fondly in *Long Walk to Freedom* of the role that running played in his formative years.

VII

The temperature is climbing through the seventies already, though it is barely light. The dry air takes the sweat off the skin. I am trying to cover ground without working hard. A low work rate is more important than hitting any particular pace. Still, five-minute kilometers are eight-minute miles and I'm able to stay fairly close to that pace even though I know I won't be carrying it all the way to the end. My last road marathon was eighteen months ago and easily under that pace but that was a year of much higher mileage. And, well, I'm older. And this race is nine miles beyond the marathon distance. And then there are the hills, and the heat, and…yeah. And for once in my life I am in Africa, and I am going to finish this race, and it really isn't about time at all.

The course map showed "feeding stations" every few kilometers. I am in for two surprises. The feeding stations have water and electrolyte, and these are the critical issues. But the electrolyte is blue Power Ade, my old nemesis. But that's it. Only liquids. No food on which to actually feed. I haven't loaded up on packets of energy gel or filled my pockets with Oreos or Fig Newtons as I would have done for a run this long.

The second surprise is that every serving of liquid is sealed in a clear plastic package like a fast-food serving of ketchup, only larger. This assures that the water is safe to drink but I have never handled anything like these packets. Even at McDonald's I have difficulty using them gracefully and that's when I'm standing still. I see others biting through the tube and neatly drinking every last drop, then flinging the plastic to the ground. I try it and can't bite through. Then I hook the tube with my canine teeth and give it a yank. It tears open and all the water flies away from my mouth rather than into it. I try another, and finally bite through again only to soak the runner next to me with blue Power Ade. I apologize and he tells me the right way to do it, in heavily accented English. You flatten one end of the tube with your thumb and forefinger and squeeze the liquid away from you, then bite through the flattened part, and squeeze. That works like a charm.

As the race goes on I discover that you can take three or four, or five, or six of these tubes with you from every station, drink a few immediately, and then carry the rest for a kilometer or so until you are starting to feel dehydrated again, or simply get tired of carrying them. They are outstandingly portable and each contains just about the right number of swallows, maybe six ounces.

It takes a long time to get to Fish Hoek, yesterday's lunch stop. Today we are eating up miles. That is a good thing, but everyone around me is running at practically the same pace so we are still in a pack without a great deal of separation even after well more than an hour. Nobody is in a hurry to start passing other runners. With False Bay on our left we run down the road past the beach, then take a right and head over towards the Atlantic.

The next miles pass through an area I had ignored from the bus window yesterday because it is a relatively flat stretch of green space between the civilization of False Bay and the challenge of Chapman's Peak.

At the halfway point a woman is calling *"Aardapfel"* and holding a box with low sides containing pieces of boiled potato in salt. Lots of runners are partaking of them. I take about four, sop up all the salt I can get, and eat them slowly over the next mile. The taste of salt is heavenly, because we have been running for nearly two and a half hours. Despite a light sea breeze, the temperature is creeping up through the seventies. My time at the halfway point is encouraging but I have no illusions about keeping up this pace. The first half of the race has been almost perfectly flat, the weather has been cool, and nobody has been working hard. The second half has the hills, and as we turn towards Chapman's Peak the easy part is over.

The talk quiets and the climb begins easily as the road turns west again. We run looking towards the Atlantic, the mountain above us on the right and a sweep of beach below and to the left. Most runners are now into a run-walk-run mode and even the running is slow. The road turns north and climbs, and suddenly we are in a signature Two Oceans moment high upon a line of cliffs etched into the side of Chapman's Peak. Far below us is Hout Bay, blue in the morning sun, a million sparkling wavelets doing nothing but move with wind and gravity while we push ourselves up, up and around curve after curve only to see yet another upward stretch ahead. Costumed feeding station volunteers, many cheering for specific teams, have staked out spots along the climb. Any thoughts of sticking to a certain pace definitely perish on the long grade, and yet another climb awaits in the miles ahead, Constantia Nek. After a very long time the grade starts to get easier, and eventually the top of Chapman's Peak road is reached. We are well past twenty miles already, and now it is downhill time.

Downhill grades are normally a treat for me, a chance to let it go and make up time, but today too many miles remain ahead. Most runners are taking the downhill very carefully saving their quads, and that is what I choose to do too. Of course carefully for me is not all that careful, and on the less steep stretches it's easy to relax and speed up a little. After five kilometers of this the road eventually comes all the way back down to sea level and into the town of Hout Bay. Smoke from barbecues wafts across the course, thick with sausage and steak odors. Parties are in progress. Small crowds of spectators cheer as we pass through into a pleasantly tree-shaded section of road on the way back north to Cape Town.

Suddenly an arch of balloons appears in the distance, marking the 42.195 kilometer point, the full marathon distance. The watch says 3:56 of race time has elapsed and my legs question whether I will make it in under four hours. Vanity suggests that I speed up in order to get a better time. Some sort of voice on my other shoulder says, "Yeah, and if you do that you will have to walk from Constantia Nek to the finish." I choose to keep up a slow stride and make it under the arch in 3:59, feeling not at all like Roger Bannister. A chip mat records the time.

The temperature feels close to eighty even in the shade. Yesterday we cruised here in a bus, taking in the scenery and marveling at the bicycle-escorted Friday runners as they ran up this hill towards the finish. Today, the going is a lot harder, and I have a new respect for the way they strode smartly up Constantia Nek, well beyond the full marathon distance. Those runners are probably at religious services this morning, if they can get out of bed at all. My devotions consist of taking walking breaks and reflecting deeply on the fact that I still have over two hours before they close the finish line. How fast, I wonder, how good must those at the front be, those who contend for the gold medals? Gerd Thys runs and wins internationally. How good are those just a step behind him who are running for the prize money here? What are their stories?

The Constantia Nek climb begins and everybody around me is walking. At this time of day in our place in the race little would be gained from trying to jog a few steps. A dedicated power-walking pace will even pass others. The leaders must have run up this slope nearly two hours ago, maybe even throwing in bursts of speed to try to gain a psychological advantage. A look at my watch suggests that the silver medal time is unrealistic. A check of my legs tells me that from this point on, any strategy is all right as long as it keeps me moving forward. The top of the hill finally appears, with volunteers handing out, improbably, sweet gooey chocolate bars. In the heat they are not appealing. I would trade a hundred of them for another *aardapfel* with salt. I need electrolytes, fluid, something designed for endurance running, instead of sugar. Few seem to be actually eating it, and for the next quarter mile dropped chocolate bars cover the road, doing an excellent job of retaining impressions of the soles of running shoes.

The heat continues to climb. And with it, appreciation of another Two Oceans amenity, tables with deep tops of the sort that you would fill with crushed ice and stick pop bottles in, except here they are just filled with cool water. The technique is to run up beside the table, make a scoop out of your hand, and splash the water all over your head and shoulders or wherever it hits. It would be nice if the road after Constantia Nek were flat, but it is not. The grade is rolling, the scenery beautiful with groves of tall trees. We pass the entrance to the world famous Kirstenbosch Botanical Gardens, and still the road winds and rolls.

Now nearly everyone around me is in run/walk mode, but the running part still feels good. The only problem is that I have simply run out of fuel. The blue Power Ade is having a really adverse effect on my system. I have only been drinking it when I can tell I am low on electrolytes, but now that is all the time. I don't know what is in that stuff, but I would give a lot for a glass of something else right now. Another runner encourages me, "Just keep running, run from the waist." Easy to say, and I try it for a while and get maybe half a mile before it's time to walk another hundred paces or so. I can see I won't make the silver medal cutoff at 5:30, but I can also see something else. I'm going to finish the Two Oceans, it will be in less than six hours and they give you a bronze medal for that, and nothing is going to stop me.

The final three kilometers are beside an expressway with virtually no shade. Simply put, it is now very hot. The finish is at the University of Cape Town rugby ground. Noise can be heard ahead, the trees thin out and the sun beats down. At the last water station the volunteers have hoses and are cheering continuously. Now a palpable sense of excitement surges among the runners. We are all going to finish and we know it. In the last kilometer the crowds along the route are thick, the route swings through a gate and onto a grass surface. A long grassy home stretch, two hundred yards through the roped-back crowd to a distant yellow banner at the finish line and I can't quite maintain the effort to sprint the whole way as I had wanted to, but suddenly there is a finish line and a clock that says 5:45. An attractive young woman puts a bronze medal around my neck and I can stop running. I am soaked. The temperature at the finish is 35°C and I calculate several times to realize that yes, that is 95°F. You wanted to run in Africa? You've got to expect some heat.

It turns out that the men's winner is Isaac Tshabalala, also the winner in 1993. The second-place finisher states that he was running to earn money for his mother's funeral. The women's winner, for the third year in a row, is Angeline Sephooa.

There is a hospitality tent for international runners, and I can see several of various races in there eating and drinking. After ten minutes or so it is too hot inside and I spend the next half hour happily watching others finish. As the 6:30 mark nears, a thick surge of runners arrives, having timed their efforts to make it just under the cutoff. Then comes one unfortunate one man who is halfway down the green home stretch when the gun goes off and the finish line is closed. He stops right where he is, a hundred yards short of 35 miles, removes his running shoes, and walks off the course into the crowd. They mean business here.

Afterwards, our little group holds an extensive post-race discussion. Two did not make it to the five-hour marathon cutoff. Another was eight minutes ahead of me, and four more made it between 6:00 and 6:30. Incredibly, one is flying back tonight to be at work on Monday. Others are going to Victoria Falls, or to nearby tourist sites. I am flying into the Kruger National Park on Monday, and will spend another week in the country including visits to Pretoria and Soweto.

VIII

Thursday after the Two Oceans. I am confined to a car, resting my tired legs for several days and driving around Kruger National Park where walking is forbidden and dangerous. The immense park, the size of Massachusetts, is home to a tremendous variety and number of wild animals and with patience I have seen and eagerly photographed the "big five," elephant, lion, leopard, rhino and cheetah, but also herds of giraffe, ground hornbills, ostrich, wart hog, wildebeest, and the list goes on, down to eagles, snakes, cranes and dung beetles.

Leaving the park on a country road, I find myself on several occasions having to skirt vendors in the road who wanted to sell me carved wooden animals. The same carvings have been on sale in Cape Town and Kruger, and are produced in factories, but there is something sad about the separation I feel. These earnest young African men are trying to stop a speeding car with a single white driver in order to make a few rand. I have the resources to be driving the car in the first place, ten thousand miles from my home. I would like to help them. I do not really want what they are selling, but there is more than that. Acting out of fear but also out of inconvenience and knowing that I cannot help everyone, I do not stop. And I feel bad about that as well, as I drive on to Nelspruit.

At dawn the next morning I am awake. Time to run. Out the hotel door and into the countryside of Mpumalanga where the sun rises. Long shadows of dawn framed with the dazzle of morning light show off the silhouette of myself on the African grass. Intense visions of being white, being black, being American, revolve and mix in my head as the roadside passes underfoot. Morning is a haven for running, a time before the business of the day arrives to complicate. Two hills away from town, a small school offers a dirt soccer field and a place to stretch. Choosing a different way back just for the challenge proves longer. Farmers in trucks pass on the way back into town, with a wave. Those walking by the road acknowledge with a look, no more.

In Pretoria, the sun rises each day as well. The broad tree-lined streets and parks are wonderful for running, and the many government buildings offer long looping roads for mileage and views of the city. My first morning there, I run with a cardboard box camera as the morning light falls across the national flag, and the door to the office of the President of the Republic. Looking out across the city from stone balustrade, I am aware of two young African men doing the same. Guards are arriving for work. Nobody bothers me or them.

Later on that day, I book an afternoon tour of Soweto. An acronym for "South Western Townships," this community arose as a home for black workers forbidden to live in neighboring, white Johannesburg. It now is home to a vast population, said to be four to six million people, over 99% black. My guide and driver is a serious young African man named Linda. He has a girlfriend and they have a child, and he is giving tours for a living. Linda shows me the yard where stolen and recovered cars are impounded, and comments that the cheapest way to get set up in the taxi business is to "arrange" papers of ownership of a mini-van in the yard by negotiating with the police that guard the entrance. The road into Soweto is busy with mini-vans headed to or from Johannesburg, and I realize why car-jacking is such a common crime in that city.

At the entrance to Soweto stands a large, bustling college campus, VISTA University, but no visible shops or business buildings. Instead, vendors line the way with wares tied up in cloth bundles that they can take home with them at the close of the business day. There is a street of opulent homes, including that of Desmond Tutu. Neighboring areas have been built of row after row of four-room brick houses, including that of Winnie Mandikezela Mandela, open for visiting and tours. Other districts are broad areas of shacks cobbled together from corrugated metal and assorted building materials, and I am invited to go into one and chat with the owner, a middle-aged woman named Annie. She is articulate, pleasant, and answers all questions graciously. Here the water is from a communal tap by the road, electricity is iffy, with little hope for anything better unless the government is able to provide it. Annie's son is in the yard sitting on a folding chair, studying for an entrance exam to a vocational school program. He has tried to enter in the past and has not been accepted. Annie hopes this time will be different, but does not appear optimistic. At least he is home studying, she says. The talk with Annie is an arranged part of the tour and I am glad to pay her for her time and hospitality, knowing that all around me are a hundred thousand Annies getting by through child care, domestic work, peddling, or whatever works.

We stop at a monument to Hector Petersen, the black youth killed in demonstrations against a government attempt to impose Afrikaans as the language of instruction for blacks. A collection of children's art related to apartheid and oppression is on display nearby in trailers. Linda asks me if I am finding the tour enjoyable. I sense a sardonic edge in his meaning, a challenge to reply. I am the one with the means to travel to Soweto to see where he lives with little. He is the black man, driving a car for hire while the white chooses to run on a holiday. We both know the situation, and he is telling me it is my turn to contribute something to the relationship between us. Only the truth is appropriate, and it will not do to pretend I am not a tourist. The truth, I tell Linda from the heart, is that truly learning is enjoyable, even if I don't like what I am learning. To myself, I add that I am grateful for Linda's unvarnished approach to Soweto as it is, a place rich with history and more than enough challenges in hand.

On the drive back to my lodging in Pretoria, Linda tells me

he is taking classes to try to get a better job. Eventually we settle into a physics debate about the nature of speed, momentum, and work. He feels that a large truck traveling at the same rate as our small Ford should have more "speed" even though it is going to get to Pretoria at the same time that we do. I try to explain why the truck needs a larger engine to push its mass at the same speed, and as I do so it strikes me that he has a point. The truck does have more something, but it isn't exactly speed. Perhaps his view is valid in its way, but it isn't going to get him past a physics exam. He is having to learn more than physics, though, because he doesn't have the relative luxury of starting from a familiar concept (speed or mass) to learn a less familiar concept (velocity, momentum, or work). The remainder of the short trip I spend trying to explain speed without confusing my guide, and hoping that I'm having some success. My best wishes, and a goodly tip, go with him. I hope that somewhere he and his girlfriend and their children are finding life better each year.

IX

Outside the window of the plane, South Africa slips into the night. The enchanting voice of Sibongile Khumalo floats on the in-flight stereo. The new South Africa is something I could not have imagined without going there and opening my eyes, and yet I have seen so little. The currents of the two oceans do mix, and the peoples of the land they wash no longer are held apart by legal restrictions. There is equality before the law, just as there is equality in a foot race, yet life clearly is not a foot race. Life in South Africa is still about race, only with the hope that it will become less so with time.

In the U.S.A., we have tackled racial justice in our way, and yet the goal has not been achieved for so many because we still live in communities and mistrust people of other colors. The planet is the process of "shrinking" and someday may be so small that all races live within arm's reach of each other, and then we'll all have to figure out how to get along. In South Africa, that someday is now. The past is very recent memory, and in many places the perpetrators and victims of former apartheid policies are walking down the same sidewalks. University students now, in 1999, were in middle school when Nelson Mandela was freed, in high school when the first elections were held. The national universities, all of them, even Stellenbosch, now are organized to teach classes in all eleven national languages.

The country has an education system that at the top is very good, but access to the top will elude most of the tremendous number of young South Africans. My heart is hopeful for this young, enthusiastic country with so much energy and promise. And at the same time my head tells me that if I were the President of this country I would be building schools all across the land, in townships and villages, cities and squatter camps, as fast as I could put one brick on top of another. The future of South Africa is right here, right now, and the land is crying for learning, economic opportunity, and a vision of a future.

There is friction even in water, however. Were it not so, all rivers would instantly flow to the sea, and all the seas would be the same. The human oceans that flow together in South Africa retain their own character even as they mix, pulled towards a future of amazing diversity and loyalty to a home and a past.

Although Mandela's term as President saw a great number of African people elevated to positions of responsibility in government and society, the sad fact is that the lifting of *apartheid* has not immediately altered the divisions in South African society, erased the differences in education or health, or created economic equality. Few Africans can ride on Mandela's coattails. Many will experience violent crime first hand, many others HIV or poverty-related health problems. All are affected by economic reality.

Even the great Mathews Motshwareteu, whose performances in the five and ten thousand meters electrified his country in the 1970s and who went on to be U.S. cross country champion at UTEP, would not be immune to the harsh realities of life. On November 2, 2001, two and a half years after my Two Oceans run, Mathews Motshwareteu was shot and killed in a robbery at his job at a second-hand car dealership. He was 43 years old, and left a wife and four children.

BOOK BAG

Any book bag for South Africa must include Nelson Mandela's marvelous autobiography *Long Walk to Freedom*, one of the hundred most influential books of the twentieth century according to the New York Public Library. I do not disagree with that assessment.

Antje Krog and Charlene Hunter-Gault, *Country of My Skull* (about the Truth and Reconciliation Commission)

Alan Paton, *Cry the Beloved Country*, *Too Late the Phalarope* (novels), and other writings

E. A. Ritter, *Biography of Shaka Zulu*

Class notes from History 381, "History of Africa" and Oceanography 431, "Physical Oceanography," Oregon State University

Stephen Francis and Rico Schacherl, "Madam and Eve," syndicated comic strip appearing in the Johannesburg newspaper *Mail & Guardian*

Europe

This fifth-century B.C. urn in the Archaeological Museum of Mykonos features the classic depiction of runners in competition.

Athens Marathon
Marathon, Greece, to Athens
November 2001

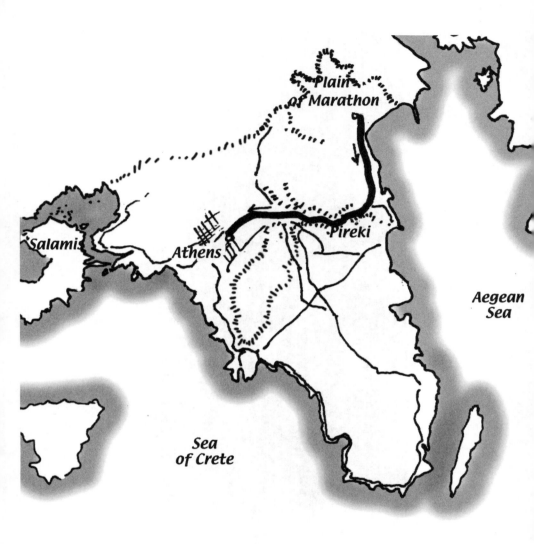

ATHENS:

The route of the Athenian army after the victory at
Marathon on September 10, 490 BC, is also the route of
historic pro-democracy marches, of the Olympic Marathon
in 1896 and 2004, and of the Athens Classic Marathon
run annually.

CHAPTER 6

The Iron Storm

Athens, November 2001

> *Their cry of war went shrill from the heart,*
> *as eagles stricken in agony*
> *for young perished, high from the nest...*
> *Yet someone hears in the air, a god*
> *Apollo, Pan, or Zeus, the high*
> *thin wail of these sky-guests and drives*
> *late to its mark,*
> *the Fury upon the transgressors.*

Aeschylus, *Agamemnon* (tr. Richmond
Lattimore)

I

History is writ large in September, 2001. The New York City Marathon in November will be a spectacularly visible part of the city's healing process. Not for me, however. The daughter who originally encouraged me to "Come out to New York and do the Marathon" has migrated elsewhere for a year to pursue acting opportunities and I will not have a free place to stay in the Big Apple. Entries into the New York Marathon can be postponed for a year. I can therefore run somewhere else just as easily. Somewhere on a continent I have not yet run.

Europe has more major marathons in capital cities than anywhere else in the world. London, Paris, Stockholm, Prague, Venice, Rome, Barcelona, Dublin, Seville, Moscow, Helsinki…the list goes on and on. All are easily accessible, festive, cultural, and enjoyable in their own way. Just make reservations, get on the plane and go. With all of that to choose from, I look at the calendar and choose Athens.

The 2001 Athens Marathon is on the same day as New York, so there will be no training schedule adjustment. The real reason to run Athens is history. The course is that of the original "Marathon," from the Plain of Marathon to the 1896 Panathenaic Olympic Stadium in its hillside grove of cypress trees near the center of Athens. Only one road goes from Marathon to Athens, meaning that the race is run literally in the footsteps of Pheidippides, whose legendary run in full armor brought Athens word of victory over the armies of Darius the Great of Persia in 490 BC. The first modern Olympics in 1896 featured the first "marathon" race on this very course, and it will again be the Olympic marathon course in 2004.

In classical Greece, amateur runners came from lands far and near to participate in sacred games at Isthmia or Delphi or Corinth. The familiar image of a pack of male runners striding barefoot and naked across the curved red skin of an ancient urn still exudes the joy and intensity of competition, in the best running days of one's young life when it seemed that life can never grow old, never end. Many of those urns are older than the legend of Marathon itself.

II

Night departure. Alchemists have turned the mighty flow of the Columbia to light. Lampglow bathes the streets of Portland, though most of the city is asleep. The new airport terminal is spacious. Hanging gardens of green trees and growing vines recall Babylon. Out on the runways, blue and green signal fires light the way in and out of the aerial harbor.

The great ships are no longer made and rowed by slaves but powered by great engines fueled with pitch and built by employees, and routinely take voyages that rival Apollo. Before sunrise my ship will reach the far shores of the ocean where Odysseus wandered. One can now fly from Athens to Troy in an hour, Rome to Carthage in minutes. The entire span of the classical world, Persepolis to Marathon or even Macedonia to the Indus, can be crossed in less than a night.

Dawn in New York. Armed guards with automatic weapons eye every passenger. Plainclothes security personnel are visible. It happened less then seven weeks ago, on just such a morning. My flight to Greece does not leave until this evening so I have the day in the city. There is only one place in all of JFK airport that will check baggage, but no attendant is at the counter and the posted rates are exorbitant. Today I do not have the heart to complain – who in this shocked city would want to accept a stranger's baggage at this time?

A bus to the train station, then a subway ride through Brooklyn and into Manhattan. The New York City Marathon is only a few days away and the exposition is already open. The walk from the subway to the expo is about five blocks but with a heavy bag and no slave to carry it for me I am obliged to stop and rest several times.

The Javits Center is vast as an airport, a temple to commerce. Once inside the center they will check bags if you are a runner, and I have my entry ticket. A long wait in line to get in and everyone is searched. Then it all happens very fast. International runners go that way, others go to the far table, here's your goody bag and T-shirt, thank you, go to the desk by the white balloons. Check your chip number, is this your name, good luck in the race.

The whole thing is efficient and feels dreamlike because I am here not to run but to defer my entry until the following year. I am going thousands of miles away to run another marathon on the same day. The faces of these runners are fascinating and I watch them openly. Jaws are set, eyes focused, brows lightly knit, heads high, the serious faces of heroes. Some are first-time marathoners who have dreamed of this for years, others are veterans trying to improve their times. All look as if they are already in the middle miles of the race and aware that the pain will set in soon. A sculptor creating a marble statue of any one of these people would love to capture his or her face at the check-in desk.

Festive music, commerce, bustle on all sides. Holding my receipt for deferred entry next year, I reclaim my bags and head out into the sunshine. Chartered buses are arriving and disgorging runners in tour groups at the curb, and leaflets are being handed out for shoe stores. On the way back to the subway I step into an art deco diner and order coffee and an omelet. An unkempt young man next to me is telling his troubles to the middle-aged waitress. "So, after all that work they just gave the part to someone else?" A sigh. "You've just got to keep yourself going, keep working and go to some more auditions, is all I can tell you." Her accent is thick New York, his could be from anywhere. The lunch, with sales tax and tip, is expensive.

I have one more stop to make. The subway goes south into lower Manhattan. The instant I step onto the platform at Chambers Street the air is different. One step through the turnstile and onto the exit stairs, and the smell of ash in the nostrils is intense, acrid. Above ground, large green barricades prevent getting any closer. One stands and looks. Up. Straight up at the open space in the forest canopy left by the felling of two giant trees, up at the ash-covered walls of the surrounding buildings, up …at the pile of rubble and twisted girders familiar from the television shots, astonishingly nine or ten stories above my head, even now.

The world has seen the images; here is where it actually happened. Several dozen others stand silently, looking upward, replaying mental images, imagining agonies. Now and then the sound of jet engines overhead. Someone takes a snapshot. The fires are still burning. The ashes cling to window ledges and facades of buildings that have been declared closed. Human remains are being discovered every day, pieces of human beings lying where they had no intention of ending.

Time crawls along between two and three on a Thursday afternoon. Today, life is astonishingly normal, boldly disrespecting the evidence on all sides that time stood still for millions, and stopped altogether for thousands, less than two months ago. The chugging of heavy equipment, the clang of metal are heard from within the work zone. I try to get a photo of the others who are there to look, and cause a palpable stir of discomfort, causing me to abandon the idea. It feels sacrilegious to turn and leave, morbid to stay. There is little to do but a lot to think about at this tomb that was never intended to be a tomb, for heroes who would rather have had their lives back than been heroes.

III

A second overnight flight in two nights. After carrying my bags through Manhattan the day before, sleep comes easily. Thoughts of those on the hijacked planes seven weeks ago have crossed my consciousness, of course. It would be futile to try to keep such thoughts out, or to deny the terror that would arise were I to find myself in the same predicament. Everyone on the plane must have the same thoughts. One rationalizes. Although the Airbus we have boarded is fully loaded with fuel, Olympic Airways surely would not be a target, would it? With security tightened, we are safe, aren't we? Fatigue sets in and the sustained drone notes of the turbines lull the mind to sleep over the Atlantic.

The flight intercepts dawn somewhere over France and in the hubbub of unnaturally early morning there are Alps outside the window. Then the Adriatic coast delineates the rugged land that is Serbia, Croatia, Bosnia, the troubles down there invisible in the morning sun from thirty-five thousand feet. Clouds appear, hiding the hardened hatreds from battles fought in the 1300s as well as the fresh scars from battles fought in the 1990s. It's time to brush up on history before we land.

The date of the historical Battle of Marathon appears to have been September 10, two thousand four hundred ninety-one years and one day before the attacks on New York. The Persian attack was no surprise. The fight had been brewing since at least 499 BC, when Ionian Greeks with Athenian help had risen against Persian control. The Ionian island areas tasted short-lived success until they were subdued four years later. A punitive Persian expedition against Athens had been mounted in 492, but turned back when the fleet foundered in storms off Cape Athos in the northern Aegean. Darius the Great of Persia, however, remained intent on imposing his empire on Athens.

In the intervening two years, the Persians had sent envoys to Athens and Sparta asking for a token tribute of "earth and water" as a sign of submission. The Spartans decided there was enough earth and water at the bottom of a well for their envoy, and tossed him in. The Athenians hurled their envoy from the Acropolis to his death, and even went so far as to kill the interpreter who translated his request, for the crime of defiling the Greek language.

In 490, the Persians arrived in force with ships designed for amphibious landings. First the island city of Eritrea was sacked after a short siege. Then the forces turned to the Greek mainland. That there would be a battle was certain, and once the Persian cavalry had landed on the plains of Marathon, northeast of Athens and on the other side of the peninsula, the location was certain as well. The plains afforded the cavalry ample room to race and maneuver.

That Pheidippides was a great runner is not in dispute. It was his job in the Athenian forces to run when running was called for. As the Athenians massed on the hills above the plain, Pheidippides was dispatched to ask Sparta for assistance. Some sources say that he got to Sparta in two days, others that he ran the round trip, some 450 kilometers (281 miles) in three days. Sensing a likely defeat, the Spartans sent back the message that they would agree to come but could not do so for another six days due to religious reasons, and did not in fact arrive in time for the battle. It is not clear how much recovery time Pheidippides had after the round trip to Sparta, if indeed he did run the round trip, but it seems unlikely that a mere twenty-four miles a few days later could have cost such a runner his life.

Other stories say the runner was actually an Athenian named Eukles, who first ran *to* the battle site because he was late, and then ran back with the news, perhaps to gain some glory with which to hide his embarrassment. The philosopher and grammarian Heraclides Ponticus is said to have identified the bearer of the news of victory as Thersippos of Eroia. But even that account would have been written no earlier than 360 BC or about as far after the event as I today am removed from the American Civil War. Whether it was Pheidippides or someone else who made the run to Athens, and whether or not anyone shouted *"Niki"* (victory) and then died, the run from Marathon to Athens and the name of Pheidippides have been evoked time and time again over the centuries as powerful symbols of Greek history and culture, of a victory of democracy over despotism, and of athletic performance in which a human runner both bears the flag of his or her origins and transcends nationalism in the name of sport.

The battle itself was fought on the plains south of the modern town of Marathon. Every account I have found relates that the Athenians attacked early in the day and swiftly, in a running phalanx that closed the last two hundred meters of open ground so fast that the Persian missiles were of little use. The center of the Athenian line was intentionally thin and was initially beaten back into a retreat that prompted the Persian forces to counter-charge. The battle then went according to the Greek plan as the powerful left and right of the Athenian lines collapsed on the center (double entrapment) with deadly force. The Persians turned and ran, by some accounts fleeing into the swamps in the northern end of the plains and by other accounts going to the beaches. In either case they were sitting ducks for Athenian spears, and though the accuracy of Herodotus' histories is questioned in many respects, his total figures of 192 Athenian dead and 6400 Persians are widely quoted in historical accounts of the battle of Marathon. That is over thirty-three Persians for every Greek, and assuming that a number of Athenians in the center must have perished in the initial charge the rout itself may have been even more one-sided than that.

There is a story that Ionian defectors from the Persian lines had come to the Greek camp the night before with news that the cavalry was elsewhere at that moment. The vaunted Persian cavalry may have gone on maneuvers in the mountains, or have re-embarked and been on shipboard, but did not figure in the battle and the lightly armed infantry that remained in the Persian positions was clearly no match for the disciplined Greek *hoplites*. All accounts I have found also agree that the bulk of the Persian forces were not destroyed because many remained on the ships throughout the battle. Knowing that Athens was undefended the main Persian force had planned to head around the peninsula by sea to strike the city itself.

Now is where the Pheidippides story comes in. The most widely heard version is that he ran in full armor at what would by then have been midday, back to Athens to shout "We are victorious," and then died. I have often wondered what kind of fool would run twenty-six miles (or twenty-four) in full armor. Now, having run the distance myself many times, I have answered the first part of that question to my own satisfaction but the armor part has remained an issue. One plausible explanation from a guidebook is that if a Greek soldier had been seen running without his armor the populace would have assumed the worst and panic would have spread faster than even the legendary Pheidippides could run. The armor signified that the home team was in control.

The fact is that no runner by himself was going to be able to hold Athens against the main Persian forces who were at that moment on the way to attack by sea. The citizenry had been instructed to man the battlements to make it appear that the city was defended, but the critical issue is that the entire Athenian army had to run the distance from the battlefield to Athens, with armor and arms, and do so in time to take up positions of defense before the Persians could get there. This all had to occur within the space of hours, for the standoff at Athens took place on the same day as the battle of Marathon and September days in 490 BC were not any longer than they are now. The Persians arrived by sea, saw that Athens was defended and, not eager for another difficult battle on what was already a bad day, turned and sailed away.

There are those that say that Pheidippides did not make the run at all. They may be right. It may be that he was among the first to get there, or that someone did die on arrival, but in a sense it really doesn't matter. If we need to ascribe an individual achievement to Pheidippides the man, it seems likely that he did make the much longer run to Sparta and back. As for the run from Marathon to Athens, it is certain that the Athenian army ran that distance in great numbers in a matter of only a few hours. For this reason I prefer to think of "the marathon" in general or the Athens Marathon in particular not as commemorating one runner's effort, but as a pack run with thousands of entrants, possibly not all in full armor and running at different speeds. Certainly they ran without numbers on their shirts (numerals as we know them not having been invented yet), but it must otherwise have been rather like the scene that occurs in any major city when the gun goes off and the race is on.

On the day itself, of course, many of the 192 heroes probably perished in the center of the Athenian line during the initial charge. Time for them stopped suddenly, at the moment they fell on the point of a spear or under a club. Those who fell never knew whether their efforts mattered or what course history would take.

Some of these were not even Athenians, but Plataeans who were on hand to assist in the defense. It is said that one of the 192 Athenians in the Tomb of the Heroes is the brother of Aeschylus the playwright. Aeschylus himself fought at Marathon, when he would have been 35 years old. In his maturity he penned the historical dramas of *The Oresteia*, heavy with a sense of morality and noble tragedy in the Greek national tradition and now part of the foundation of Western literature. Long after Marathon, Greeks would speak with pride of an ancestor who fought in the battle. The epitaph of Aeschylus mentions that he fought at Marathon and ignores his literary successes.

And of course because history is so often written by the victors, we know nothing of the six thousand four hundred men in the vanquished forces whose lives ended in the swamps and along the shores of Marathon. This was a substantial part of the Persian forces, estimated at twenty-five thousand by some, and well more than twice the death toll at the World Trade Center in 2001. Each of these soldiers had a childhood, a family back east in Persia or Scythia or Syria or somewhere, and plans for what he might be able to look forward to once this Athenian business was cleared up. Many were probably impatient at waiting on the plain, elated at first at what appeared to be a suicidal charge by the Greek defenders, then puzzled at why no Persian cavalry appeared to save the day, then finally confused, terrified, disoriented in flight, and eventually knew if only briefly that the only question remaining to be answered in this life was whether it would end by arrow, by spear, or by water, and how long it would take. Certainly few of these men awoke that morning expecting their lives to end by midday. And nobody knows what tales they would have told had they had the opportunity.

One thinks of the battle of Marathon as having "saved" Athens. This is true enough in that if the battle had been lost, Athens would certainly have been lost as well. But there is more to the "saving" of Athens than just the battle of Marathon. Only ten years later, in 480, the Persians were back in force under Xerxes, the son of Darius. This time the invading force was so powerful that the Greeks evacuated Athens and went to the island of Salamis, from which they watched their city burn. Thanks to the famous delaying action at the passes of Thermopylae and the great naval victory in the shallows between Salamis and the mainland, Persia was defeated again but at a great price. This time victory was not a matter of a single battle and a runner but of hard-won, coordinated, and bloody battles at a number of locations in southern Greece involving not only Athenians but Spartans and Greeks of other ally states.

Aeschylus also authored *The Persians*, a tragedy set in the enemy capital of Susa amid the shock and grief of the Persian nation after the defeat at Salamis. The classic Greek tragic formula of overweening pride or *hubris* followed by utter destruction fits well in the locale of the enemy capital, and the speech of the chorus and actors rings with the horrors of a catastrophic loss but is also peppered with homage to Greek strength, emotional fuel to a nationalistic Athenian audience. Late in the play, having writ large the agony of Persia, Aeschylus has the ghost of Darius acknowledge Greece:

> *No more against Greece lead your embattled hosts'*
> *Not though your deep'ning phalanx spreads the field*
> *Outnumb'ring theirs: their very earth fights for them.*
> (tr. Richmond Lattimore)

A comparison might be made between the defeat of Persia at Marathon and the defeat of the English in the American Revolution. Persia returned to burn Athens ten years later, and the English came back in 1812 to capture and burn the capital city of Washington. In either case, had the former conflict gone the other way, the latter probably would not have happened. But neither Marathon nor Yorktown marked the end of the victors' troubles with the vanquished. The interpretation I am most comfortable with is that Pheidippides by himself did not save Athens any more than Paul Revere won the American Revolution. Both made bold, symbolic journeys that were crucial in their way.

The footsteps of Pheidippides, or Thersippos, or Eukles, and the reincarnation of the run first as a novelty in the 1896 Olympics, then as a mainstay of Olympic competition, and finally as a milestone in the aspirations of ordinary runners striving for extraordinary accomplishments, not only echo in the rhythm of the steps of all long-distance competition, but also suggest the footsteps of Greek civilization and culture and nationhood through its many twists and turns from 490 BC to the present day.

IV

Much of what I can see from the plane window during the last hour of the flight was once Greek, or controlled by Greece in the classical era. Since that time it became governed first by Rome, and then by the city known in turn as Byzantium, Constantinople, and Istanbul. As the Ottoman Empire weakened in the nineteenth century and then disintegrated after World War I, modern Greece was recreated amid intense patriotic fever and much debate about how large the Greek nation should be, and what was actually Greek.

Greek has been spoken and written continuously, and Greek communities have existed around the Mediterranean ever since the classical era. There are long-established Greek populations in Lebanon, Egypt, Cyprus, Libya, Sicily, and now of course in places like New York as well. There may be more people outside of Greece who identify themselves as Greek than there are inside. In Greece today, it's pretty clear *who* is Greek. Everyone. Ninety-five percent of the people in this, the most homogeneous European nation, are Greek.

V

The body that organizes the Athens Marathon, SEGAS, is dedicated to keeping the event low-budget, basic and, well, Spartan. There are few amenities, no pre-race Expo. Basic organization and no more. This has led to criticism over the years as the gap has widened between Athens and the splashy, opulent, and beautifully organized marathons of other European capitals but SEGAS has steadfastly maintained its no-frills policy. This year we are told a delegation was dispatched to Boston to learn how to better organize a major marathon, but veteran marathoners are still skeptical that Athens will be anything other than a do-it-yourself effort for most runners any time soon. The attraction to this race continues to be that there is only one Athens and only one road from the place called Marathon.

My little group of runners is staying at a cozy hotel near the Plaka, the old tourist area in the heart of the old city. We are escorted to the Acropolis and to the 1896 Olympic Stadium and other sites around the city by a wonderful guide with a rich command of English and the mind of an art historian. The days before the race are overcast and breezy, not the azure blue of postcard scenes of Greece but promising for distance running.

Race day dawns stormy, however. Rain has been falling all night and is now coming down hard and heavy. My small group piles onto a bus and heads out of Athens along the very course we will be running back in a few hours. There is little early morning traffic as we pass the embassies and offices along the major boulevard towards Marathon. The route rises steadily, meaning our last miles will all be downhill. At the crest, a flyover bridge under construction requires yellow barriers forcing traffic to squeeze around the excavation. We will have to squeeze too.

Outside of Athens, it is still raining hard and the bus splashes through several small rivers of water crossing the road. Each splash produces expressions of dismay on the bus. It will mean wet feet, heavy, uncomfortable feet. Soon we are in farmland, amid olive groves and winter vegetables. Far off to the right lies an arm of the Aegean Sea, iron-gray beneath the stormy sky. Then near the modern town of Marathon, the bus slows and sloshes axle-deep into a sea of brown water filling the entire road and into the fields. A wake of brown waters rises on either side. Genuine groans from the runners. This is no stream crossing. There are no detours. The race will have to go right through it. Well, this is a trip you make perhaps once in a lifetime, and today is the day for us to be here and this is in commemoration of a true feat of bravery. One does not turn back because of a little water on the roads. At least we don't have to fight a battle.

We disembark more than an hour before the start, at a small soccer stadium that will serve as the starting area. It is still pelting rain, and windy as well. Just plain cold. The soccer field is too sodden to run on. The buses announce that they must leave for Athens before the road gets clogged with traffic. All non-race gear must be put on the buses, so it will be available at the finish. But how are we to stay warm in just our racing shirts, for an hour until the start? Drivers and organizers shrug. That's the way it is. Apparently the only way out of this storm will involve going right through the middle of it. By the hundreds, runners begin improvising solutions, huddling together or scavenging plastic bags and wrappers from the trash containers that are filled to overflowing from a recent soccer game. This provides a source of very crude windbreak attire.

With about thirty minutes to go we are told to assemble in the stadium, and do so. With twenty minutes to go we are told to assemble on the road, and do that. Then abruptly, we are instructed to assemble again in the stadium so that we can parade to the start. Once all the runners have filtered back inside, nobody can figure out who is supposed to assemble where. Most of the runners are Greek, but they don't seem to understand the instructions any better than I do. This situation, so to speak, is Greek to me and the English translation isn't much better. Wasn't it an Athenian interpreter who got killed in 491 BC for the crime of defiling a language? In a few more minutes we are still a cold, wet, unruly mob of runners and are attempting to again pass out of the single-file stadium gate and back into the road for the start. One benefit of this confusion is that it keeps us moving and therefore slightly less focused on how cold we are. Someone is handing out sprigs of laurel leaves. I take one and tuck it in a vest pocket. Too late it occurs to me that I could have taken ten.

Suddenly it is seconds to go before the start. One young Kenyan in a bright gold shirt is trapped far back as the pack begins to press forwards towards the starter. Someone notes this with alarm. With shouts, we make way. The pack parts like the Red Sea in acknowledgement that the Kenyan belongs at the front. He looks like, well, a Kenyan marathoner, which is to say a genuine potential world champion. Like every other Walter Mitty back in the pack I would love to have his speed and stamina if only for one race, and I am secretly hoping that he becomes famous. I will then say I once made way for him at the start. I'm sure that by the time I finish my race he will be showered, fed, and well into a post-race nap or even on his way to the airport for the return flight to Nairobi.

The gun goes off, and with rain slanting towards us from the Aegean we are off in the steps of Pheidippides. The Kenyans are out ahead immediately, dark arms and legs and bright gold shirts easily visible as they pull ahead of an otherwise mostly Greek and European race pack. Feet pound the hard, marble-like pavement. Bodies start to warm with exertion. Many runners have been wearing extra shirts because of the cold conditions and lack of shelter at the start. Now layers of clothing are being shed at the roadside. With the air temperature above 50°F, I am immediately warm. It is obvious that I won't need my ratty old turtleneck, already so soaked with rain that the weight of the added water is a nuisance. To take it off I have to shed a light poly vest, then shed the shirt, then put the vest on again, all while running. This challenge keeps me occupied for nearly a mile. Then the shirt falls beside an olive grove, perhaps in the very place where an Athenian warmed to the task of running and shed a stained battle tunic.

Barely three miles into the race we reach the deep water. Brown and flowing, it covers the road for at least fifty yards and approaches knee-deep at the center. Muddy banks and rain-soaked vegetable fields line both sides. More water is falling from the sky. Some runners have chosen to detour through the fields of cabbage rows, but the mud there is at least a foot deep and they do not look happy. Others are simply splashing their way through, soaking socks and shoes completely with twenty-three miles yet to go. I have a couple of plastic bags scavenged from the trash barrels at the soccer stadium, and stop to tie these around my legs. I wade in hoping for dry feet but within three steps find that it doesn't work. Waves kicked up by other runners swamp the plastic and the bags become buckets of dead weight around each foot. So I hop out of the bags. Both shoes are immediately filled with icy brown water. Nothing to do now but chop ahead through the flood along with the others. Within a dozen splashy steps the water rises above mid-calf, chilling the legs. Keep churning, lift the knees, go forward, lift the feet clear of the water surface and lunge ahead, splash back into the cold mud, lift the other foot and do it again. Can't stop here, no matter how bad it feels. And eventually the lake does start to get shallower and the strides get easier.

Back on the pavement I have to keep moving to prevent my chilled legs from cramping and to force the water out of my shoes. This was certainly a dirt road in the ancient days, perhaps with ruts from carts or chariots, but the surface today seems to have marble chips in it and feels as hard as a tile shower-room floor. It takes another five minutes or more of squishing along before it feels like the shoes are again snug against my feet and I can run comfortably. The trials of Odysseus come to mind. I wonder if there will be a Cyclops waiting in some upcoming kilometer. Oh, Divine Homer where is your "sweet west wind, singing over the wine-dark sea"? Another look at the weather coming off the Aegean gets me a faceful of rain out of skies more evocative of Winslow Homer.

I wonder what sort of footwear the Athenian *hoplites* wore. Nike may have smiled on them – the actual Nike, of course, the goddess of victory – but they couldn't possibly have had cushioned insoles under their feet. Perhaps they would have envied my Asics running shoes, even soaked with flood water. This strikes me as an excellent time to remember that I'm here to retrace footsteps and to finish on my feet, not to make a certain time on the clock or to beat any other particular runner. It is all about Greece, and it is also about democracy and heroism and history. That's a lot to think about and I've got a long way to go.

The great playwright Aeschylus, himself a veteran of the battle of Marathon, wrote of the Persian wars:

> *Then has the iron storm*
> *That darken'd from the realms of Asia, pour'd*
> *In vain its arrowy shower on sacred Greece.*

Times may have changed, but the iron storm is still with us.

Two generations after Marathon, Pericles stood before the people of Athens to deliver an oration during the Peloponnesian War. According to Thucydides, Pericles was well aware of the difference between talking and doing, and was not comfortable making a speech to honor deeds: "I should have preferred that, when men's deeds have been brave, they should be honored in deed only.... Then the reputation of many would not have been imperiled on the eloquence or want of eloquence of one."

In other words, don't talk. Do. Get out there and run. Here's to you, Pericles, today we are not cheap cardboard imitations of Pheidippides on the road with the news that saved Athens. We are on our feet, in action, doing deeds that recall deeds, filling our lungs with air freshened by a storm off the Aegean and tackling this road for no other reason than that it is *their* road, the road they died to defend, the road that Pheidippides himself had to have run because it is still the only road back to Athens.

And in this run where thinking about history is appropriate, I find that there's so much to uncover once you scratch the surface. To be honest, I didn't know a lot about modern Greece before this trip.

The Athens of Pheidippides, and Aeschylus and Socrates and Pericles, lasted less than a hundred years after Marathon before a devastating plague. The Athenian culture of that day continues to influence thought in the West and beyond even now, but it wasn't the only culture in Greece. Athens fought wars with other Greek states frequently during that time and eventually was swallowed up in the empire that was being built by Alexander the Great of Macedonia. Athens became an early part of the Roman Empire, in which Greek culture and thought were highly regarded (recall that at Julius Caesar's funeral, Cicero spoke Greek, according to Shakespeare). The New Testament was authored in Greek in the first two centuries AD. The Eastern half of the Roman Empire centered in Constantinople was culturally Greek and survived for centuries, becoming Christian in the fourth century and in the process extinguishing the practice of the Greek religion. Later in history, the lands of Greece as well as the Greek communities in cities around the Mediterranean and Black seas were ruled by the Ottomans, but retained Greek communities, churches and civil institutions. The Ottomans considered Greek to be more an identity than a location. Greeks everywhere were considered part of the "millet-i-Rum," which was in general the Orthodox Christian religion and community.[8] This system lasted into the creation of modern Greece in 1820–31 and the subsequent working out of the nation's modern borders after World War I.

---

[8] There were other millets in the Ottoman system, an Armenian millet, a Jewish millet, and so on.

Sources differ as to the degree of separation among people of the various millets in daily life, but I note with some pride that one role in which Greeks served the Ottoman empire with distinction was that of dragoman or official interpreter. From their positions in commerce and finance in various cities of the empire the Greeks were a naturally polyglot community. As the empire's interface with Europe grew in importance the dragoman profession attained a position of considerable distinction. This came to an end with the Greek war of independence in 1821 after which the Greek dragomans in all parts of the empire were seen as potential supporters of a Greek cause and the system was revised. The loss of so many skilled interpreters

The marathon pack strings out, past more olive groves and farm lands. The rain eases up, then pours again, driving in from the sea off our left side. Rivulets of water are everywhere on the hard pavement. There are aid stations every few kilometers featuring tables groaning with too-large bottles of water. Each bottle is at least twice what a runner should drink in one go, and more than I would want to carry with me. Someone told the committee to have plenty of water on hand, and the message must have been copied to the weather gods as well. But the Greek gods have a sense of humor, or at least irony. The only electrolyte drink available is my old nemesis, blue Power Ade. This is the sugary stuff that I had far too much of during an ultramarathon in the heat of Cape Town. I delay drinking the blue liquid as long as I can, maybe ten miles, then decide to give in and go for it and hope my stomach holds out. There is considerable time to think yet, for we are not yet even halfway.

The legends of Marathon imply that Greece was victorious, Greece was re-created...But what was Greece, even then? Athens and Sparta were intense rivals. Were they not both Greek? Sparta temporized to avoid sending troops to reinforce the lines at Marathon, probably smelling an impending defeat. But Sparta,

---

caused an administrative crisis but also led to the establishment of an Ottoman diplomatic service.

The millet system in Ottoman times was in a way echoed more recently in the modern Lebanese constitution, which attempted to formalize a balance among the country's religious and ethnic communities. Following a complete census in that country in 1932, roles in the government were allocated to different sectors of the population more or less in perpetuity. The President's office was to be filled by a Maronite Christian, the Prime Minister's office by a Sunni Muslim, and the speaker of the Chamber of Deputies was to be a Shia Muslim. The Port Authority of Beirut was by consent to be run by a Greek. It was not a fully democratic solution nor necessarily balanced, but guaranteed a representation of major parties and intentionally prevented any one of them from gaining complete control over political and economic life. It is probably not surprising that actual government power has not always fallen along those lines and political strife in Lebanon continues to this day, but in

like Mycenae, Corinth, and Argos, was there to defend Greek culture when Persia attacked again ten years later. The informers who snuck into the Athenian camp the night before Marathon with word that the Persian cavalry was away were Ionians and therefore Greek, but had been working for the enemy. Perhaps "Greece" back then was more like Yugoslavia in the latter twentieth century, a concept that for a while made compatriots of bitter enemies. Perhaps the divisions were like those in the Islamic world today. The nineteen attackers of the World Trade Center were, in their own eyes, devout Muslims, yet many more than nineteen Muslims died in the attacks and most of the Islamic world was horrified.

So maybe it isn't such a simple thing to design a nation around a culture, or to agree what the geographic boundaries of that culture are, or to expect that members of that culture won't squabble among themselves. I wonder how many other Ionian Greeks were in the Persian lines and fought against the Athenians at Marathon? How many other states like Sparta did not send aid to the Athenian side? The twenty-four-mile run of Pheidippides and the rest of the army was heroic, but how much of Greece did it really represent at the time?

Modern Greece needed unifying forces and symbols, and in everyday life the most powerful of these were of course the Greek church and the language. The journey I am retracing from Marathon to Athens this Sunday morning, however, has also been

---

this constitutional arrangement is also the sense that communities continue through time and have a role in civic life, and that one of those communities is Greek.

Modern Greece was reconstituted in the 1830s following the war of independence, and its territory was defined in terms of the geographic footprint of Greek culture. Unlike Germany and Italy, which were created by internal fusion, the powers that participated in the making of the new Greece were not states within the new nation but the major European nations of the day. Not to put too fine a point upon it, there are parallels to the U.N.'s role in the creation of Israel in 1948.

the site of at least two highly visible and emotional events that became symbols of Greek national tradition in the modern era. One of these is the first marathon of the Olympic Games. The other is an event I will learn about the morning after the race.

So many miles, so many footsteps. Was any runner ever luckier, any athlete ever more at the right place at the right time than Spiridon Louis? A number of good running books, like those by Charlie Lovett[9] and David Martin,[10] tell the story of the first Olympic marathon and I'm not going to try to improve on their research. But it's still a great story and there's no better time to recall it than on a rainy day when one happens to be running from Marathon to Athens.

Spiridon Louis was not the first to run the course or the distance, or the fastest in his country's team trials, or originally even on the team. Usually described as a shepherd from the village of Maroussi outside Athens, but also variously as a postal carrier, soldier, or a farmer, this young man made the list of entrants into the first Olympic Marathon race as an afterthought.

The idea of a novelty event to commemorate the legendary run of Pheidippides was proposed to Baron de Coubertin, the founder of the modern Olympics, by Michel Breal, a French philologist (and therefore arguably a translator). With the race to be held on April 10, 1896, a test run from Marathon to Athens was made by two Greek runners in February. The first of these to finish, according to Lovett, was a G. Grigoriou in a time of 3:45, and a Giorgios Grigoriou is in fact listed among the seventeen starters of the Olympic race. Lovett's account states that the first qualifying trial was held on March 10, and was won by Kharilaos Vasilakos in 3:18, followed by Spiridon Belokas and Dimitrios Deliyannis. These three are also listed among the starters. It was

---

[9] Charles C. Lovett, *Olympic Marathon: A Centennial History of the Games' Most Storied Race.* Westport CT, Praeger, 1977, pp. 3–8.

[10] David E. Martin and Roger W. H. Gynn, *The Olympic Marathon: The History and Drama of Sport's Most Challenging Event.* Human Kinetics, 2000.

then decided that there should be more runners in the event, and in a second trial just a few days before the race, Spiridon Louis finished fifth. That performance would hardly place in a university meet, but Lucky Louis was on the team, one of thirteen Greek runners who would start the race.

There were at least five foreign hopefuls, but as Lovett relates, the Italian Carlo Airoldi, a professional distance runner who had traveled nearly a thousand miles by foot from Italy, was barred from competing under the rules of strict amateurism. Airoldi in my mind gets considerable credit for traveling to the Games in the classic manner, passing through foreign borders on foot in the name of sport. He may well have won the race had he competed.

The four foreign entrants who did start included three who had already won medals in the 1500 meters. These were Australian Edward Flack, a London resident who had also won the 800; Arthur Blake of the United States; and Albin Lermusiaux of France. They were joined by Gyula Kellner of Hungary. That meant there were thirteen Greeks out of seventeen runners, pretty good odds for a country that was thirsty for a home-town win and a symbol of national athletic pride on a world stage.

The four foreign runners had the track speed and the medals to prove it, but were probably in the race on a lark, none of them having competed at a distance even half as long as the marathon before. The Greek runners, on the other hand, had all run the course, even though some had done so only a few days before. By all accounts the race was nothing like a typical modern marathon competition with a lead pack of runners going out at something like the same speed for at least half the race. Perhaps trying to recoup some glory lost in the 1500, Lermusiaux tore off at phenomenal speed and in Lovett's account is reported to have reached the village of Pikermi, just over halfway through the race, in 55 minutes and with a two-mile lead. By my calculation that would be over twelve miles at a pace of just about 4:30 per mile, equivalent to two back-to-back 10K races in 27:50. Considering that Haile Gebrselassie's Olympic record set in 1996 was 27:07, this performance of Lermusiaux is either world-class, or exaggerated. At that rate, I calculate that the three other foreign runners, two miles behind, would have been moving at a 5:30 pace, still very fast for marathon neophytes who according to Lovett had never raced beyond ten miles.

By now I too am reaching Pikermi in the race. There is a church service in progress, bells ringing, a crowd of people outside the doors looking at the stream of runners splashing towards Athens on the Sabbath. Smaller clumps of spectators huddle under awnings or beside walls. The trees afford no protection from the rain. The road begins to rise gently, steadily. The wind no longer cools me, for it is at my back and the road is rising to meet my feet, bringing to mind the old Irish blessing. Not a blessing for runners. In 1896 the American Blake dropped out shortly after this point. Maybe he knew something I don't, but today I am going to at least improve on his performance. Lovett recounts that Spiridon Louis, reaching Pikermi far behind the leaders, "enjoyed a glass of wine and expressed his certainty that he would win the race."

The hill also began to eat at the pace of the Hungarian Kellner, who was passed by the first of the Greeks, Vasilakos. The slow climb gnaws at my pace as well, and the blue Power Ade is eating at my insides. I have some gels and some food in my pockets, and ration these for extra energy every kilometer or two. I know I am perspiring but I am so soaked with rain that it's hard to tell how much water I actually need to drink to remain hydrated internally. Externally I am so hydrated it isn't funny. We are now in the third quarter of the race. The final quarter will begin at the crest of the hill and from there it will be all downhill to the stadium.

Lermusiaux, though slowing dramatically, managed to hold his lead all the way up the hill to Karavati, where after a couple of falls he called it a day at twenty miles and surrendered the lead to the Australian, Flack.

For my part, I too am falling farther behind on the hill. Near me, a group of Greek students in gold shirts is running in formation and chanting something. They gain on me, pass me, and then slow down for water and I pass them back. They are not fast, but they are a spirited team. The only other people I am passing are those who have slowed to a walk, but not many others are passing me either. There are pleasant-looking groves of trees and gardens and some fairly nice houses along the road, as well as shops and stores. The climb from Pikermi to the top of the hill takes me a good hour and by the time the crest is in sight the field of runners has become a loosely connected string with large gaps. We weave to the side to get around the construction. My insides are in turmoil and I spy a portable toilet and make a much needed stop, during which time the pack of gold students passes again, still chanting. A few hundred more yards of hill and it will be all down. And I count myself a fairly good downhill runner.

Though not a household word in world track and field, Edward Flack deserves recognition as the first Olympic champion at both 1500 and 800 meters. Of the three non-Greeks who medaled in the 1500 and started the marathon, he ran the farthest and held the lead the latest in the race but like the other two, he would not finish. Somewhere after the crest of the hill Edward Flack was overtaken. Not by Kellner, nor by Vasilakos, nor by the other Greeks selected in the first trial, Belokas or Deliyannis, but by Spiridon Louis.

Spiridon Louis must have put on a burst of speed up the seven-mile hill. Perhaps there was something in the wine in Pikermi, or maybe this twenty-four-year-old shepherd had velocity that he simply had kept in reserve during the second trial run only a few days earlier. Perhaps he had known that he only had to finish that trial run to be selected for the main event. At any rate, with less than six miles to go he was dueling Flack for the lead and all accounts agree that the scene was tumultuous as Greek spectators hungry for a win in the games cheered him all along the boulevard winding down into Athens. A cyclist had already been dispatched to the stadium to announce that Flack would win; now a second cyclist was sent to announce that a Greek was in the lead, and the stadium erupted in celebration. Lovett relates that Flack, "unable to catch him, staggered and fell and was carried from the course." Vasilakos was now in second place, although well back, and Belokas was running near him in third.

Back on the boulevard I am finding the going miserable. I had counted on the downhill to be a place that I could at least stride comfortably, but the miles in waterlogged shoes, the cold rain, and perhaps the digestive issues as well are causing my legs to cramp. Not ordinarily prone to cramps, I am unsure how to deal with them. The rain continues to fall, and we are now in Sunday noon city traffic, with police at every intersection blocking drivers who are upset at being delayed on their way to Sunday dinner. The phalanx of students in gold is just ahead of me and I resolve that I will at least pass that bunch before the finish, but the fatigue continues to build.

Louis entered the newly refurbished white marble Panathinaikos Stadium at the open end and ran the final lap accompanied by no less than Greek Crown Prince Nicholas and Prince George, who then carried him to the royal box. Not a bad day at all for an unknown twenty-four-year-old shepherd. He received a medal, and the commemorative silver cup donated by Michel Breal, as well as a genuine ancient vase with a picture of a runner on it. And more than anything else, Spiridon Louis received a place in the hearts of his countrymen forever. He was a guest at the 1936 Olympics in Berlin, and he died in 1940. I have not found any account of his ever having run another race, and in a sense he did not need to. Perhaps as a coincidence, the 2004 Olympic Stadium is being built in his home town of Maroussi, now a suburb of the city of Athens. The 2004 Olympic marathon, however, will end in the marble Panathinaikon amid the cypress trees, where Louis finished and where I am going to finish, no matter how lousy I feel and how long it takes.

With a mile to go the course passes a large statue of a marathon runner made entirely of stacked plate glass. That is about how I feel at the moment, but the knowledge that there is only a mile to go is welcome. Today there will not be a good time on the clock because, cramping and now cold again, it has been all I can do to maintain a shuffle on the downhill slope of the boulevard. The rain and wind have kept anyone from overheating but when things start going bad the chill just makes it worse.

Finally the stadium comes in sight and to my further annoyance we are asked to run a couple of hundred yards past it and then back up the road to the entrance. Once inside, the track is spongy and pleasant and I am too tired to imagine Pheidippides shouting anything and perishing, or seventy thousand Greeks cheering for Spiridon Louis. I pass the finish, accept a space blanket and a medal and a finisher's certificate in Greek and happily slow to a walk, then sit for a few moments in the rainswept marble grandstands to watch others come in.

The moment of the finish is personal, for some a short sprint and an exclamation of joy, for others just a quiet arrival at a point in space and time and an inward sigh of relief. National battles are not being won today, only personal contests. An elderly man comes in dressed in the colors of both Greece and Turkey. Some marathoners run for ideals. Quietly I ponder my own motives for taking on this particular run. Partly it has been a need for a journey, for a deed in honor of deeds and journeys. It has not come off as planned, but I have finished the race anyway and in so doing have added my one little pebble to the now towering cairn built by all those who have run this course, with greater or lesser glory, or any other marathon, over the centuries. Of the seven continents, this is the only race in which I have not broken four hours but at the moment I am only too glad to stop running.

The race has been won by a Kenyan, to no surprise. He has led us through the rain and the flood water, and appropriately his name is in fact Noah, though he is not the young man that we helped get to the front at the start. Well done, Noah. May you run again and again in your country's colors. For the rest of your life you will be known as the first to reach Athens from Marathon on this day.

At length it is time to rise from the cold marble bench and walk back through the park. A young Greek runner catches up to me and in uncertain English tells me that this was his first marathon. I muster all the praise I can find and let him know that he's a hero. We talk of future races. He'd like to run Venice. I'd like to run Istanbul, and he grudgingly admits interest. Our paths diverge and it's time for me to get out of the weather. The shower is hot, the dinner is excellent and, as always, there is no sleep like the sleep after a race. But I am not done learning about the significance of this road from Marathon.

VI

On the morning after, my little group goes for a loosening-up run to the top of a hill opposite the Acropolis. It's a windy, dry day with scattered clouds and the spots of sunshine are welcome. Eventually we go down to the tiny office of SEGAS to see if we are in any of the race photos (I am in one, and duly purchase it), and someone looks at the name of the race on the official sweatshirt. The name on the shirt is the same as that of the figure on the reverse side of the finisher's medal, Grigoris Lambrakis, a name not known to me until I do a little research. And what I uncover astounds me.

On April 21, 1963, a Marathon March was held amid student demonstrations and popular opposition to election rigging. The march was conceived as a popular demonstration for democracy. The choice of the route itself and the act of going from Marathon to Athens, to preserve a democratic tradition of government, were deeply symbolic. The authorities banned the march and arrested several thousand people. Grigoris Lambrakis, one of the leaders, was also a popular sports figure, having been a champion runner at the Balkan Games. This did not protect him but he was also a parliamentary deputy and therefore enjoyed legal immunity from arrest. As marcher after marcher was arrested, Lambrakis finished the march alone, gained considerable media attention, and thus became an instant hero in the student movement against totalitarian government.

The government did not take this act lightly. Only a month later, after another peace movement meeting on May 22, Lambrakis was run down by a car in the middle of a Thessaloniki street and fatally wounded. He died on the morning of May 27. The following day some half a million people accompanied him to his grave, many shouting slogans in favor of democracy and invoking the name of Lambrakis. Government involvement in his assassination was immediately suspected and eventually discovered.[11] Three years later, on May 22, 1966, thousands of Greeks made another peace march from Marathon to Athens to commemorate the third anniversary of Lambrakis' assassination.

Here in November 2001, I have just run in an Athens Classical Marathon also organized in memory of Lambrakis, himself now a symbol through his determination to finish his "marathon" alone, literally in the face of the forces that wished him dead and within five weeks would get their wish. Pheidippides, Spiridon Louis, Lambrakis. Heroes do not die. All of these heroes went from Marathon to Athens, and all were Greek.

I vote with Pericles. I would not honor my heroes in word; it is much more appropriate to honor their deeds with further deeds of my own. Actions that would honor Pheidippides and Lambrakis would be actions in favor of democracy, rule by the

---

[11] The following account is from www.mikis-theodorakis.net. On May 31, 1963, in an article in the daily *Athinaiki* the composer and activist Theodorakis wrote *"It's a law that assassins drown in the blood of their victims. ...By picking on Lambrakis as their victim they have chosen their judge and their avenger. A single Lambrakis is more than enough to send them all to their graves. Lambrakis is lost but thousands of Lambrakides have been won – thousands of suns which will keep him alive and illuminate his memory."*

The following month Theodorakis was elected president of the Lambrakis Youth, and the following year he was elected to Parliament as a representative from Piraeus. That same autumn Theodorakis wrote the music for which he is probably best known in the West, the score for the film *Zorba the Greek*.

deimos, the people. Large numbers of people. People who seldom stand united or agree with each other, of course, unless and until something brings them together. And even then they can expect opposition. In New York, the rallying cry is "United We Stand," and at the moment this is palpably true. At the Tomb of the Heroes of Marathon, or at the still smoldering tomb of the innocent above the Chambers Street subway station, the beholders stand mute and united. But whom do we face, and to what end have I flown this far and run these rain-soaked miles? What deeds are appropriate, what actions can be clearly and unequivocally justified? In the meantime, I will continue to run. Perhaps the same questions burned in the minds of the ancient runners, pushing against gravity and accelerating into time, as they were watched by a forgotten artist who then depicted them in black on an old red urn.

VII

Morning, with post-marathon stiffness and more, a sense of real fatigue. Today I am again just another tourist on a bus winding through sodden late-autumn fields below brown mountain slopes to Delphi. We have all day to enjoy. It feels good to get out of the city of Athens, just as it probably has for twenty-five centuries.

Delphi exceeds expectations. Situated high on a hillside with a view across a broad valley and out to a distant arm of the ocean, its glory thousands of years gone, this ancient site was buried and nearly forgotten. Once there were scores of temples here, treasure houses sponsored by all of the city-states and islands of the Greek civilization, thousands of statues and wealth beyond description. Though the lands of Greece were buffeted by wars and the making and breaking of empires, this city of temples built around the oracle remained sacred and powerful for centuries until Christianity came to the Byzantine Empire. Theodosius is-sued a decree to destroy all pagan idols at the end of the fourth century AD, with the result that Delphi was abandoned to the elements. Around the same time there was a ban on non-Christian festival days that effectively spelled the end of the ancient games of Olympus and Delphi.

In the museum at Delphi one can now see amazing examples that hint of the grandeur that once was here. The famous bronze statue of the charioteer in particular, with his youthful, confident gaze and simple draped garment, is arrestingly alive as he eyes the journey before him and holds the reins of his means of travel.

The stadium at Delphi is at the highest level of the ruins but our legs are not too tired to make the climb. The inside of the arena is about 170 yards long. The ground is sandy, with puddles of rainwater where once there must have been intense competition. Capacity crowds of 7,000 once cheered fleet young men perhaps from Phoenicia, Ionia, or Egypt as they toed the starting line and then sprinted towards glory at the finish. I hand my camera to a fellow runner and stiffly jog down and back. In this moment I am running in more famous footsteps than ever trod the surface of any modern sports stadium. Time is occupying my thoughts. I have been laboring to retrace footsteps long buried, my legs no match for those that have gone before and my dreams much less lofty and focused. Perhaps it is enough to just go home with a sprig of laurel in my pocket that was handed to every runner at the start in 2001 rather than to the victor at the finish in 500 BC. Those Kenyans who ran at the front of the pack can realistically aspire to a laurel wreath some day, to be worn with honor in Boston perhaps, but it feels as though my actions here in modern-day Greece have been simply workmanlike retracing of a journey long since ended. My mental mumbling continues in this vein when suddenly I am struck by the opportunity for glory. The bus has stopped at a souvenir shop in Delphi and there, in the window, is a replica of an ancient vase with the famous marathon runners on the side. There is only one. Taking pains to appear calm and not betraying my excitement I wait my turn to get off the bus and try not to knock anyone over as I stride into the store and over to the show window. There it is, behind a stack of fluffy throw rugs. One quick grab and it's mine, and I wouldn't trade it for Spiridon Louis's silver cup. Sure enough, the signature on the bottom says fifth century BC for all the world to read. Several other runners see it and their envy is so palpable that I pick out one of the rugs that wouldn't look too bad at home and wrap it around the vase. Taking care not to set it down or let go at any time, I get my trophy wrapped and stashed in my travel bag where it fits with no room to spare. Suddenly the rain on the course, the four-hour time, the disorganization of SEGAS and ruination of the glory of Delphi are less burdensome. *"Niki!"* Victory has smiled upon me at last. In the shiny new Athens airport before departure, a fluorescent overhead advertisement features a picture of the Greek marathon runners. From a vase just like mine. Black-on-red, they strain joyfully towards an invisible finish line. The product is most un-Greek, Heineken beer. The road from Marathon, the games and wars of Greece, are etched in the global collective unconscious now. Few games or wars since have produced heroes more immediately recognizable than the black runners on the red urn. May they still be running, and may there still be human runners like me to appreciate them, 2,500 years from now. My race here, however, is done. Time to cradle my carry-on bag with the replica urn snugly wrapped inside, head for an airport bar, order a Greek beer instead of a Heineken, and await the launch of the great ship that will carry me home.

Book Bag

Aeschylus, collected plays, primarily *The Persians*, also *Agamemnon, The Eumenides* and *Choephoroi (The Libation Bearers)* (translated by Richmond Lattimore)

Charles Lovett, *The Olympic Marathon*. Praeger, 1997

David Fromkin, *A Peace to End All Peace: The Fall of the Ottoman Empire and the Creation of the Modern Middle East* (primarily sections dealing with Greek history after World War I)

South America

A pickup soccer game in the parks of Florianopolis. The player on crutches to the right of the goal became part of my inspiration for running the marathon despite a foot injury.

Maratona de Santa Catarina
Florianopolis, Brazil,
September 2002

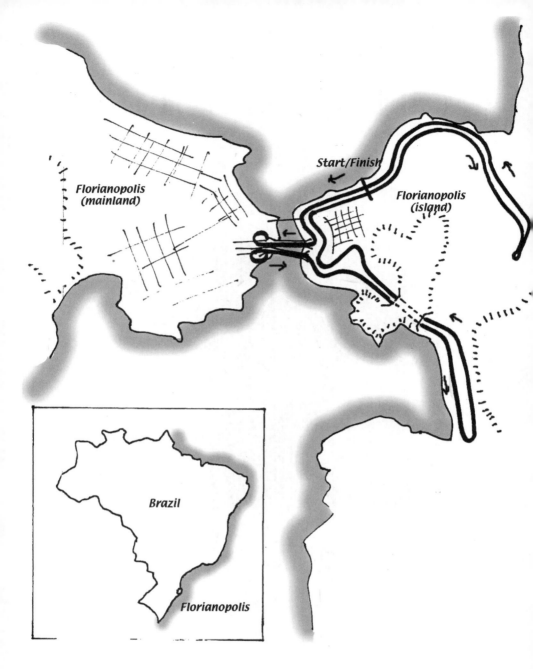

Start/Finish

Florianopolis
(mainland)

Florianopolis
(island)

Brazil

Florianopolis

FLORIANOPOLIS:
The route of the Florianopolis Marathon as it was run in
2002, starting and finishing on the bay front with trips west
to the mainland, south on the new expressway, and northeast
to the University district.

CHAPTER 7

Heads Up, for Now

Florianopolis Marathon, Santa Catarina
State, Brazil, September 2002

> *"Running a country is like running a marathon. You*
> *can't set off at top speed because you'd be out of breath*
> *by the first corner. You must take sure and deliberate*
> *strides in order to end your term in office certain that*
> *your obligations have been met. And I want to be able*
> *to tell the world: how good it would be, how marvellous*
> *it would be if instead of the rich countries making and*
> *spending money on so many arms, they spent money on*
> *bread, beans and rice to stop people being hungry."*

Speech delivered by President of the
Federative Republic of Brazil, Luiz
Inácio Lula da Silva, at the World
Social Forum, Porto Alegre, Brazil, 24th
January 2003

I

A legendary city, a Brazilian island, a reunion with an old friend, a miracle. That should be enough for a great story any time. The truth may be a little more prosaic than the words sound but yes, it all happened. I was there.

I have this thing about finding coins. I can't remember where I got the idea, but I will only pocket a found coin if it is heads-up. Heads means George Washington or Queen Elizabeth II, otherwise the side with an animal, or the side with the primary artwork or if I can't tell any other way then the side with the year of coinage.

A shiny silver dime in a Seattle parking lot, a scuffed five-yen piece on a Tokyo subway platform. Fragments of value according to custom, just a tiny gain to the finder. Useless in any other way. Well, the five-yen piece with its hole in the center actually makes a great lamp cord pull. But these are symbols of opportunity found. If the coin is heads-up I keep it. If it isn't heads-up, I will turn it over. And leave it heads-up for the next person to find. A deeply symbolic act. A profound philosophy. Take that which is appropriate to take. But also inspect, improve, and leave genuine opportunities for others.

The odds are elegant. Heads or tails, equally likely. Half for me, half for the rest of the world. But who knows, the next three in a row might be for me.

The great thing about real luck is the feeling that it leads to more luck. Opens doors, and switches on the lights for other lucky things to happen. Gets the whole world running in a lucky direction. Getting into a good college, finding a perfect soul mate, showing up just as the "Help Wanted" sign is placed in a window, all promise more luck. I suppose winning the lottery would presage more good luck because there would be all those dollars to spend on good causes, but I've never won the lottery and don't know anyone who has. As far as the lottery goes, I'm the lukewarm optimist that buys a ticket occasionally but never checks to see if it won.

Life isn't a lottery, but luck in life does exist and should be taken seriously. Enough luck, usually small, comes along in life that you can recognize it for what it is. And sometimes, maybe only a few times for most of us, you'll get into some real luck of the kind that changes your life and maybe even more.

Luck began to happen in July 1999 when we heard of an exchange student from Parana state in Brazil, who was without a host family. As it happened we had only an eighth-grade daughter at home, and a free room. Raquel moved in, bringing Brazil into our family circle. She is a brave person, as is any teenager who chooses to live a whole year as another family's child, in another culture, in another land. Raquel is such a hero. There were intense highs and lows. There were silences and laughter, tears and smiles. At first, when her English was shaky, we played cards together. When her backpack and journal were stolen, we all felt hollow and angry. But by later in the year we were able to chatter together in English for hours, and even her journal was found and returned by the police, and somewhere during that year Raquel became a member of our family for life. It was with genuine regret that we waved goodbye a year later.

The river of life has days that aren't sunny, however, and with time the clouds begin to move in. One of my running companions was diagnosed with Parkinson's. A shy, quiet cousin chose to end her life; none of us had known she had leukemia. A sagging economy affected my self-employment, and finances slid into the trough with it. Old career disappointments began to stain my thoughts with bitter jealousies over what might have been. Children graduated, accelerated into young adulthood, my wife's career soared, and soon I could tell the nest would be empty.

By late 2002, other changes are taking place. Denial is not an option. A dramatic slowing of the metabolism, a longer time before my heart rate can settle into a long-distance pace, knee and foot pains that just won't clear up. The late "Indian summer" of my early fifties had brought some good race times and the exhilaration of training with a younger local runner who made it into the U.S. women's Olympic marathon trials, but it is clear those days are over for me. Blood tests are normal Heart, normal. Diagnosis, as feared, normal. Just getting older. I know I am running out of time to be carrying the training load required to run marathons under four hours. Six continents are not what I set out to run, though. There is one more remaining.

I have no idea where I would want to run in South America. The major cities are mostly either hot and humid or hilly or at high elevation. Hills, heat, and altitudes are the hardest conditions for me. So Caracas and Lima (hot), Quito (9,000 feet elevation) and Santiago (5,000 feet) are not attractive.

A web search turns up a site in English with six or seven Brazilian marathons. Rio, it turns out, has been cancelled Sao Paulo I know is crowded, sprawling, and that marathon is at the wrong time of year. Recife? Vibrant culture but very, very hot. Curitiba? Legendary for creative and environment-oriented urban planning, and the capital city of Parana state, but the Curitiba marathon is described as hilly, the toughest in Brazil. No thanks. Ah, here it is. Florianopolis. Island city on the southern coast. Weather cool enough. Course newly altered and flat. Ocean views. A short bus ride from Curitiba. Race date in September, usually the best time for me at the end of the warm, dry Oregon summer. Fares to Brazil are cheaper after the U.S. summer holidays are over. Punch my ticket.

II

Summers in Oregon are beautiful, dry and warm, and 2002 is no exception. Trails and forests, roads out by the airport for longer days, friends for shorter noontime runs. My favorite spots are there for me: the top of Bald Hill, the return from the creek trail offering a sweeping view of the valley to the snow-topped Cascades, the tall firs of the university research forest.

The recipe I have used in past years begins to work. Increase distance at first, don't worry about time or weight loss. Throw in occasional track sessions for fun and a challenge but don't force the pace because the ultimate goal is a marathon. Eventually the weight loss begins, bringing a little more speed and a sense that longer distances will be possible. The confidence that I have learned how to do this, thoroughly, makes it easy to build condition and run each day.

A few races serve to increase the sense of excitement, including one summer ritual that I cannot pass up. A friend offers me a spot on the Hood to Coast Relay, a weekend of fun for teams of twelve runners covering nearly two hundred miles. It will be my eighth Hood to Coast. In the past I have relished the intense downhill speed of Leg 1 where the race starts by plunging down the side of Mt. Hood, dropping over 2500 feet in five miles. This time, however, I have too much at stake to risk an injury. I negotiate for Leg 11, long and easy, with two of my three stretches to be run on old railroad beds that will be very flat. It will be like running three 10K races in about sixteen hours, run-recover-run. Great training for a marathon.

My first leg of the HTC is run under a full moon approaching the lights of Portland in the early hours of the night, chatting with the few other runners that start late with my team. The second is in the early morning mist on a beautiful rural road. The third is in the afternoon heat, down a straight path cut through a producing forest, with many runners from earlier, slower teams ahead for me to pass. The company of other runners is exciting, my team wins an over-50 age group medal and the race has me feeling fast, lithe, and happy. Until I wake up Tuesday morning and find I cannot walk.

Something is very wrong in the middle of my right foot. I can barely put weight on it, though wearing a shoe helps somewhat. Shifting forward to take a step makes the pain worse. It doesn't feel like a sprain. A doctor X-rays the spot, but can only offer the comment that stress fractures often don't show up in film. This is not funny. I am supposed to leave for Brazil in about ten days, to run a marathon in less than two weeks.

My wife and daughter see my predicament, but also see no reason to cancel camping in the Cascades over Labor Day. And they are right. We are able to find a couple of great tent sites in spite of the holiday campers, and do all the standard stuff including marshmallows and graham crackers. By the third day I am able to slowly walk a couple of miles around Clear Lake, but still cannot run a step.

More than twenty-five years earlier, before one of the annual fifteen-mile races in Ann Arbor that were the first events I ever ran, I had developed a golf-ball sized swelling on one foot (I forget which) that forced me to stop training about a week before the race date. I had become very depressed about it, then very determined, and resolved to lace my shoe very lightly and go to the starting line anyway just to see if I would be able to run. When the gun went off, the pain vanished, and I wound up setting a personal record for the race by eight minutes. Not only that, but the injury never returned.

That sort of thing is called a minor miracle, worth crowing about. Or so I thought until I discovered that every runner has a similar story, and doesn't necessarily want to hear mine. I wrote it off to a lucky strike that I hadn't deserved, and largely kept the story to myself.

The thing of it is, at age fifty-three I have much more at stake than a local race. The ticket to Brazil is non-refundable, and there will be more expenses once I am there. I have trained myself all the way up to marathon readiness one more time, and then the ultimate question. Would I ever be in shape to run a marathon in South America again? Possibly not. The seventh continent, the whole Seven Continents concept, is probably in the balance.

We decide that it will be best for me to get on the plane and go. Even if I cannot run, I will be in motion. There will still be my other goals on this journey, to see our daughter Raquel again and meet her family, and to get a look at the urban planning accomplishments of the ecological city, Curitiba. The marathon is only a day in this journey, as on each of my previous journeys. And in a week, who knows what healing might take place?

Less than forty-eight hours before departure, I pull out every running shoe in my closet, get all three pairs of orthotics that

I own, and go to the most forgiving surface I know of, the old cinder running track at the university. I try all five pairs of shoes with each of the orthotics, fifteen combinations in all. The most cushioned shoe, combined with the stiffest orthotic, allows me to jog a lap nearly pain-free. I note the second- and third-best combinations as well, and all go into my carry-on bag for the flight. Also in the bag are a new jar of ibuprofen, which I have never used in a race before but have heard runners talk about frequently, some blue emu-oil pain relief rub, a pack of stiff moleskin with small scissors for shaping, lots of bandages and spare shoelaces.

The strategy for this race is to endure and finish, and in fact to avoid undue speed at any point. Accordingly, I also pack a heart rate monitor and several packs of energy gel. Of course, if the foot does not cooperate none of this will matter.

III

For the first time, I am going alone to a country where I do not speak the mother tongue. The visa to Brazil is free of charge, but not free. Their country imposes a $75.00 fee on visas for U.S. citizens, because that is the fee our country imposes on their citizens. It's an attitude that says clearly "We are equals." Impressed, I pay up. We are equal many times over, because in Brazil, I cannot identify myself as "American." Brazilians know that they too are Americans – South Americans. Nor can I refer to my country as "the United States." They are "The United States of Brazil." On this trip I will be "from the U.S.A."

A volume of Brazilian history goes with me for in-flight reading. But I am continually reminded of Raquel's disinterest in history. She always said it was boring. Maybe that was the attitude of a teen, or maybe it was something else. I decide to give history its place in my preparations but also to look at Brazil as it is now, a young country with a median age around twenty, an industrial giant. Brazil may have been the only American country to be the seat of a European empire (under Dom Pedro II), but it is also a land of youth. And youth live in the present.

A first-time tourist in the U.S.A. might miss a lot of history too, yet with an educated eye one could see traces of Jeffersonian democracy in a school board meeting, the legacy of the Homestead Act in the gridlike road map of the heartland, or the results of the Americans with Disabilities Act in the redesigned access ramps to public buildings. Certainly the signs of our slave trade and assimilation policies are evident in our people, and the effects of the Patriot Act in security measures are tangible. The scissors I brought along to trim moleskin for my feet are confiscated before I can board the flight. I should have known better.

Flying into Brazil I see vast *fazendas* from the air, huge expanses of coffee trees stretching in neat rows to the horizon, with cleanly drawn irrigation patterns and roads. These are major private landholdings, visibly unlike the 160-acre Homestead Act plots in the U.S.A. Tremendous tracts have been cleared and now supply Folger's and Maxwell House with beans grown in direct sunlight and bred for high caffeine content. On an earlier flight (between Buenos Aires and Bogota, returning from the Antarctic) I crossed Amazonia, three hours of trees unbroken by a single road or airstrip. I now have two contrasting visions of the center of Brazil, one the greatest forest and river in the world and the other a gigantic coffee cup.

The legendary city, Curitiba, sounded too good to be true. All right, it doesn't vanish into the mist or make dreams come true, at least as far as I know. Any city can be wonderful if you are there for something you really enjoy, but at the same time a hellhole if you are floundering and can't find a way to leave. The city of Curitiba is very proud of the way it "broke the rules" and created its unique achievements in city planning, though, and once you know what to look for the signs are evident. Eric Piel wrote a master's thesis in anthropology that describes the innovative ways Curitibans have handled the issues of urban growth. I had to see what it was all about, and I flew there. You can too.

In Curitiba are fifty-two square meters of greenspace for every resident, more than in many industrialized nations. For every tree cut, the city provides two more to be planted. Recyclable trash can be exchanged for school books, holiday gifts or surplus food from farms. Three rock quarries have been recycled into an outdoor stadium, a glass-and-tubular-steel opera house and a free environmental university. A former garbage dump is now a botanical garden tended by street and low-income children in exchange for school supplies and food. I particularly love the story of the first pedestrian mall in South America. After business owners stalled the city council vote on a Friday over the mayor's initiative, the mayor and his friends went ahead anyway. Several blocks of street were filled in and the mall created stone by stone, tree by tree by citizens literally over the weekend. By Monday, the mall was a fact, business in the stores increased rather than died, and more blocks were added as store owners caught on to the idea. You can walk on that mall today, its white stone squares a testimony to innovation for the common good.

The growth of this city has been strong, from 360,000 to more than two million in the metropolitan area at present. As elsewhere, costs are borne by corporate entities in addition to taxpayers, but the city has remained in control and so far has resisted giving concessions to developers and businesses at the expense of the general public.

Flying into Curitiba, I can see squares of developed land well out in the rural farm areas. Housing for low-income individuals is available through the *solo criado* system in which developers give or purchase land on the outskirts to be developed with water, electricity, sewage, and dirt roads. The city subsidizes prices for 30-foot plots on which families can hold title to their own property and build with city assistance. Over time these neighborhoods become much more stable than the more typical case in which poverty-driven slum migration fuels cycles of instability. Everyone benefits, including residents of the city center.

My first task on arrival is to get out my Portuguese dictionary and buy a pair of scissors (*tesaura*) for moleskin and some band-aids. My next is to go ride the Curitiba bus system.

Like many cities, Curitiba came to the point where it could build a subway. Underground systems are expensive to build and maintain, and have limited ability to link to surface routes. The city listened instead to suggestions from its bus drivers and commuters, and solved the problem its own way, building the *Ligeirinho* system at an estimated one-ninetieth the cost of a subway.

The major urban boulevards have dedicated bus-only lanes, and each bus stop is on a raised platform, like a subway. Passengers pay to enter the stop, which is a glass tube like a tennis-ball can on its side. The buses are articulated, multi-axle vehicles with entrances at the center door and exits at either end, so that riders can exit twice as easily as they enter. One story has it that the city debated an expensive electronic system to make buses stop exactly at the center of each station, until the drivers pointed out that a simple painted line on the pavement would do as well. Today, buses stop at the line.

I ride the bus system around on several boulevards. Passengers flow easily off and on during the midday hours, and the bus speeds along its own unobstructed lanes in the city. This is precisely an above-ground subway, swift, affordable and low-key. Normal bus routes run elsewhere in the city. I have read that the city converts its old buses into mobile classrooms, to educate electricians, plumbers or clerical workers in low-income areas, and into facilities for children's art and music classes. I once lived through a hot oil-boom summer in Houston, when a reported third of the city's new diesel buses were out of service while the rest crawled sluglike through traffic on congested streets. Houston had thousands of times the resources, but I would prefer to commute in Curitiba.

Curitiba has a public tourist bus that loops around a day's worth of monuments to its immigrant populations, the gardens, the Free University. At the spectacular glass-walled Wire Opera House another tourist quips that powerful singers could cause a lot of damage. Nursing the ache in my foot, I climb the wooden structure at the Free University of the Environment and listen to the frogs under the greenery below. One reads that Curitiba's most innovative days may be over, and that the city is milking its reputation as an environmental haven for maximum tourist effect. Even if this is true, this city has a great deal to be proud of and the question in my mind must be the same that other tourists leave with as well. Why aren't these ideas implemented in more cities?

During my visit, election campaigning is in progress. Tables and canopies are in place all up and down the famous mall, some crowded and active, others empty. The question hanging in the balance is whether the ruling party will be replaced by the populist candidate Luiz Inacio Lula da Silva, universally known as "Lula." In the gray, rainy spring weather of September the Lula tent on the mall is nearly empty, suggesting that he is not doing well in central Curitiba. As a former union leader and activist, however, Lula has strength all across the country.

After a Brazilian fast-food lunch it is time for the comfortable afternoon bus down to the sea coast and southward, crossing the bridge onto Florianopolis island. Hotel rooms are abundant in Florianopolis in the spring, and several touts at the bus terminal give directions. Tell them Paolo sent you. I accept a free map and head in the indicated direction, then find my own hotel with a lower price and a better view.

It is time to stay off my feet. From the hotel window, I can see an impromptu soccer match in the park. Eighteen or so teens and young men are playing "the beautiful game" with captivating panache. I will admit in writing that I played college soccer in Ohio in the 1960s and still referee at the high school level. Here in Brazil I can only watch as schoolboys effortlessly use expert moves far beyond anything I have ever encountered.

Amazingly, one of the defenders is playing on crutches, angling across in front of the goal to stop attacks and swatting the ball away with a crutch tip whenever it gets in range. The rest of the players take this in stride. He manages to get upfield quickly enough to put opponents offside occasionally as well. If that young man can get on the field and be at ease in the game with only one good leg, then I can go to the starting line tomorrow. After a couple of hours, the players take the nets down off the goalposts and go off in several directions.

IV

Alone in the hotel room the night before the race, worries begin to crystallize. I have no more time to rest my foot, little chance that I will get back to South America any time soon, and a definite sense that it is getting harder to run marathons.

I don't have the answers, but I do have a pen and a lot of paper. Taking a different sheet for each thought, I write thoughts.

And here is exactly what I write that September night:

> BIGGEST FEAR – That I'll be back in here in less than an hour, still full of too much energy and hope and with a broken foot and unfulfilled goals and no idea when I'll ever do it again and maybe be old and fat in 4–6 months and be through with running and active life in general forever.

I sign that one and put a frowny face at the end.

MARATHON RUNNER AT WORK
Back by 1:30!!!

This is the familiar sign I put on my dashboard whenever I'm out for a road run and parked where anyone might question or tow my car.

M. L. P.
1952–2002

My quiet, perceptive cousin who passed away a few months earlier. My fears are vain in comparison with reality. We are all lucky to be here, those who run tomorrow and finish, and those who don't.

A journey, a run. Both start with a need, before even a single step is taken.

I have spent the last ten days not running when I ought to have been running, not preparing when I ought to have been preparing. Fearing the injury that prevents attaining the goal. The fear has been a kind of catharsis in itself, knocking me wholly out of my accustomed rituals of preparation. I am reduced to seeking a miracle, a Sunday morning when my foot won't hurt for four hours of activity that normally makes even healthy feet hurt.

So much positive catharsis sits on the one end of the scale labeled "finisher." I make the 26 miles one more time, I justify the trip as a sporting event, I finish a marathon on the one continent, South America, where I have never done this before. I become a Seven Continent Marathoner, part of a select community of sixty or seventy persons. I complete in this sense a journey I began nearly nineteen years ago, training on the banks of the Tama River in Tokyo, driving up to Kawaguchi before dawn, walking occasionally in the last miles of the race but still finishing in 3:34 under a brilliant, cold winter sun and the white snows of Fuji.

The other side of the scale, however, says "non-finisher" and I must admit that it matters very little to anyone but me. I don't make the 26.2 miles, maybe I don't make twenty, or ten, or even one. I don't justify travel on the basis of a sporting event – does there need to be a sporting event in order to travel? Perhaps I will then justify the trip as something else, something equally good, that I have been de-emphasizing in the name of sport. I may not become a Seven Continent Marathoner, but nobody other than me really cares about that and it's a crazy concept anyway.

It would be a lot of trouble to train to this point again, even though it's been fun too. In all honesty I am probably two or three years past the age at which I should be doing marathons. In other words I might never get back to this point, and I'll just have to live with that.

Hah!! I may fail but I will try, and I will try with every strategy, trick, and training mile in my entire past. And with ibuprofen and emu oil, and orthotics and good broken-in shoes. And a heart monitor to ensure I don't go too fast at any point. And a song in my heart for every runner who ever took up a challenge. And a smile for every song that ever went through my head, for the sheer good fortune that the world ever got made in the first place and that I am in it, in this day and age, and here and strong and still a bit young and able to get on a plane and do this, and for the flow of the air over wings and through turbines that can carry me to such distant beaches in no more than a night to hear the waves of the South Atlantic and the tones of Portuguese and the rhythm of the samba and the slap of a soccer ball.

I will go to the starting line because starting lines are important. I will move forward because motion is essential and new horizons are always around the bend. And because I have two strong legs and my blood pressure is 120/80 at age 53 and my resting pulse is even lower than my age. I'd even like to see how many 10K's I can do in 53:45 (my age) or better.

And because I'm me and I don't give up!!

That one sits on the table in front of me for several re-readings. Somehow, it feels right.

Then, finally:

Imagine a world where all you have to do is do your job, get paid, run, travel and be with friends. A world where whatever you do to help someone works, and is enough. Imagining such a world is a nice alternative, after things don't work out.

Things very well may not work out, no matter how well you planned them.

Your foot may undo all the benefits of eight months of training, great blood pressure, low pulse, fourteen marathons, 25 years of running and racing...and your desires.

And if it does, you have to live with it.

Until it does, enjoy the fact that you are able to be a part of this run, in the wind and weather on a far foreign shore.

Samba! Step up to the line, look at the crowd, get with those your own speed, look for soft road shoulders to run on, think of Oregon, Africa, Athens, Antarctica, Chicago, Boston, Melbourne, Kawaguchi.

And if you're on your feet at the end, thank your lucky stars. Because you do have them.

The pages are shuffled, read, and re-read. Placed together, reviewed, and finally let lie on the table as sleep approaches. The alarm is set early.

V

The gun goes off. The first kilometer or so the course runs in the "wrong" direction away from the city. Then we double back along the other side of the boulevard, getting a first look at the leaders as they turn before us, and pass the start again. I am running steadily, trying to set my foot down softly and avoid any uneven surfaces. Fortunately the pavement is in good shape, completely flat. By the time we pass the start I have a good rhythm going. The effects of the long layoff from running have me feeling like I could do this forever, but I'm acutely aware that one bad step could end everything.

We move around the bend of the island and into the city, up over one bridge across the channel and onto the mainland. I'm running easily and would be going faster except that makes the heart monitor go over 150, which is my red line for this race and means "slow down." We loop under the bridges and back to the island over the other bridge to the ten-kilometer mark, having had a second look at the leaders as they cross ahead of us. The first ten kilometers have passed in 52:30, which is indeed less than my age.

Coming off the bridge we turn south through one tunnel onto the south bayfront and along a brand-new expressway, down the unopened part at the southern end to a turnaround at 16.5 kilometers (third look at the leaders), and back up the other side. The twenty-kilometer mark is just before the tunnel coming back, the halfway mark (21.1 kilometers) just after. The sun is now direct enough that the tunnel is a relief. The heart monitor keeps sending the same message "no hurry, slow down, take it easy," and the watch is telling me that as long as I keep going I'll make it under four hours, but not much faster.

Next the course loops over a viaduct before descending onto the boulevard past the access to the two bridges we ran earlier, then back around the bend to the north bay where we started. At about twenty-four kilometers the race time says about 2:09 and I pass beside the finish line and head out for the loop to the university. In a couple of minutes the winner is coming towards me from the other direction, escorted by sirens to the finish (fourth look at the leaders). He probably finishes in about 2:15, by which time I still have ten miles to go. My heart monitor still says "slow down" and by now I can see that in previous races there has always been a point like this where I have run too hard out of excitement or simply impatience. I slow down.

A long stretch from twenty-six to thirty-three kilometers leads along the north bayfront past gleaming apartment high-rises and dark blue waters. After thirty-three kilometers we start a loop into the Federal University of Santa Catarina, which rolls a bit, the only real hills on the course other than the bridges. Between thirty-six and thirty-seven kilometers we emerge back onto the bayfront, and the heart rate is edging a little higher, the legs getting stiff and painful but the foot still okay and now it's a countdown of kilometers and minutes going back along the waterfront, a long left-hand loop until we hit forty kilometers and see the last 2.2 around the bay to that little white tent at the finish. The tent seems really far away but fortunately this is because it is very small. And in a few more minutes of stiff-legged striding, with a samba in my heart and a smile on my face for everyone who ever accompanied, encouraged, or merely tolerated my running, I try to kick in the last hundred yards and pass under the clock as it says 3:58.

At the finish line, a brief buzz as I am processed, handed a medal, shorn of my race chip, and released from the chute into a happy crowd of young Brazilians. Slowly the pulse relaxes, feet cross the grass to the water's edge. On all sides runners are sipping water, or guarana or beer, chattering and radiating the happiness of finishers everywhere. Ahead of me on the shore is a woman of maybe thirty in a *fio dental* bikini, even though the temperature is no higher than the low seventies. Brazil is in the sound and the sight and the sunshine and the light breeze, and just to be here is much more than pleasant.

And if you're on your feet at the end, thank your lucky stars. Because you do have them. I will not need any second chances. The left ankle and metatarsals have held together. No words to describe the relief, the dance on the edge of personal disaster. But it would be sacrilege to simply stride away into the beautiful dream that followed upon waking today. The doubt was deep and spoke its own wisdom, and part of that wisdom was that this event to any of us was merely a personal outing over so much pavement, and my reasons for journeying are only valuable in proportion to what I can gain from them. It was my event alone, one passage on the boulevards of Florianopolis. Let other runners find their journeys, write and dream and finish, and tell the tale to a listening ear in their home upon the return.

A plane will take me west to Londrina this afternoon, to meet some people I have been wanting to meet for a long time. On their doorstep without language skills, or plans, only a desire to go and see what lessons life can teach. Just as their daughter arrived on an American doorstep three years earlier. *Because starting lines are important. I will move forward because motion is essential and new horizons are always around the bend.*

Without knowing why, I step out of my racing shoes and slowly wade into the coolness of the South Atlantic. And gaze at the hills of Brazil stretching northward into the distance.

VI

Those who have been or hosted an exchange student know that family ties are created this way. This wonderful custom goes back decades in the history of travel. Not very long ago travel was by ship and most communication was by letter, and the student was really far from home. Today's high schoolers would call that ancient history.

I was never sure whether to encourage our Brazilian daughter to call home when she lived with us in 1999–2000. But she was only the touch of a dial away and it helped her cope with the stress of separation. By the holidays she was acclimated and chatting in English and by June it was difficult to part. Now, two years later, I am again unsure whether to go see her in her family setting in Brazil.

I should not have worried. "Our" daughter and her brother and sister and parents are warm, energetic, and fun to be with. The family is solidly middle-class and runs a small manufacturing concern in Brazil's textile industry. We tour the city, climb the stairs inside the cathedral spire, visit factories, watch TV, eat, and talk constantly. The three kids handle English really well, fortunately for me.

Life in Brazil is the same and different. A big dog for security is also just a loving puppy to the family members. Brazil has high crime rates and close-knit families. All five get by with one bathroom. Why do Americans have so many bathrooms? The family has a maid working in the kitchen five or six days a week. In the U.S.A., we have a bread maker, rice cooker, blender, coffee maker and digitally controlled stove but people are too expensive to hire. Raquel put on weight in Oregon, mostly due to stress. Since then she has since lost all of it and then some. Brazilian girls seem to prefer to look razor-thin if they can, and I worry about her. She has made it into a local university and is majoring in psychology. She wants to work with children, and this will be a great fit. She seems naturally suited for it.

The family treats me to a Brazilian barbecue, cut after cut of pork, beef, chicken, chops and steaks, more protein than I would eat in a couple of weeks. I can't keep up with the feast, but it is delicious. What is more, it seems amazingly lavish to be able to travel so far and be among a family. We have never met before, and yet we share the most personal connection. A child who has become an adult with their nurture, also with ours, and with a good measure of her own ingenuity as well. It is uproarious fun to sit together, share pictures, tell stories and crack jokes in two languages and watch this young woman and her sister and brother handle the translation impeccably.

The coin has landed heads-up repeatedly for me. My foot never bothered me again after the marathon. Apparently all it needed was twenty-six miles on hard pavement! I have a lot to be grateful for on this trip. Frequently Raquel's family refers to their painful indecision as to whether to send her, their youngest child, to the U.S.A. The finances weren't there and she was not sure she wanted to go. It was an act of faith for all of them. For now, the coin seems to have landed heads-up for her as well.

The time comes to start on the journey home, and it is a sad parting. There was a race, and I finished. There is also a tug in my heart for this family, for their love for each other, their church, their business. For the hope we all have for our children. For the hope embodied in the innovations made in Curitiba. For the future of this giant, youthful, energetic land called Brazil.

Within a few weeks of my return, Lula is elected President of Brazil. It is the first time a socialist has headed this country, a major departure from rule by the business elite and the military. Early in his term, Lula has to address the high expectations of his constituents who want everything to change immediately. He too is attempting to go the distance, and will need skill, endurance and a few lucky heads-up coins to succeed.

Within a year of my visit to Brazil, Raquel is diagnosed with anorexia nervosa. No longer in control of her body's appetite, her weight loss spins out of control. Many days she cannot leave the house, and she is hospitalized briefly. Fortunately, she is studying in a psychology program and her department knows exactly what is going on. She is allowed to rest when needed and attend class when she can. Her family and church unite behind her with powerful support. Slowly, with the help of medication and counseling, she is able to regain the ability to eat. By 2004 she is doing much better and finishes that school year in fairly good shape. Her desire to work with children remains strong, and she will now be able to counsel anyone with anorexia from the standpoint of a survivor. The coin is heads-up again for her, and we all pray that it will remain so.

Late in the summer of 2004, the Olympic Games are again held in Athens. The men's marathon course begins at the town of Marathon and follows the same traditional route I ran in 2001 finishing not in the new Olympic Stadium but in the old marble 1896 Panathinaikon. For much of the race a Brazilian runner, Vanderlei de Lima, runs in the lead, well clear of a pursuing pack of runners from several continents. Near the top of the hill, however, he is tackled to the ground by a figure emerging from the crowd, later identified as a disturbed Irish priest with a history of mental imbalance and religious fanaticism. De Lima recovers and continues running but is passed in the final miles by Stefano Baldini of Italy, and Mebrahtom Keflezhigi of the U.S.A., who go on to finish first and second. Though he has perhaps been robbed of his chance for an Olympic gold medal, de Lima enters the Panathinaikon in third place, assured of a bronze medal. Circling the narrow stadium track to the finish he smiles under the blazing lights, spreads his arms like a bird soaring, and in doing so becomes indelibly imprinted in the history of the marathon and the long list of Brazilian sports heroes known and loved as much for the way they won as for the fact that they won.

BOOK BAG

Eric Piel, *Power and participation in urban planning: an ethnographic case study of Curitiba, Brazil* (Thesis for Master of Arts in Anthropology, Oregon State University, 1997).

Erroll Lincoln Uys, *Brazil (a historical novel)*

Pele (Edson Arantes do Nascimento), *My Life and the Beautiful Game*

E. Bradford Burns, *A History of Brazil*

Epilogue

The very air is electric. Black thunderheads boil in the east, in the direction of the Fergana Valley. Broad, leafy avenues are nearly deserted. Two and a half million people remain indoors.

Life has been cheerful, pleasant for the past four months in this Central Asian crossroads of Turk, Persian, Mongol, Arab, Russian, Korean, all travelers on the Silk Road through the centuries. Food and services are plentiful and for us, cheap. Daily we shake our heads at pleasant new discoveries about life in this former Soviet sphere, words, tastes, sights, vibrant and colorful histories of new friends, ingenious confluences of first-, second-, and third-world forces. Uzbekistan is young and ancient at the same time.

An Uzbek friend had invited my wife to spend the weekend with her family in Andijan, six hours away over a high mountain pass. They were to leave this morning, but they never would have arrived. The roads have been closed. Last night, angry mobs in Andijan stormed the prison and released two thousand inmates, including many apparently held on politically motivated charges. This morning the TV channels are silent, but Tashkent knows.

I slip out the staircase of our apartment. Normally there are hundreds of people on the corner here, a small plaza with a subway stop, a large store, an ice cream stand and a restaurant. Today there is only a police jeep parked diagonally on the terrace. I avoid crossing the corner directly and cut across the bus lanes out to the wooded strip in the center of the boulevard.

Nobody in Tashkent has ever bothered me during a run. On the subway or walking on the street, I get checked for documents at least once a week, and know never to leave home without identification and a copy of my passport. Here, as everywhere, though, a runner seems to be invisible. A pair of old brown camping pants is perfect for exercise, has a pocket for the passport ID and another hidden pocket for a few dollars and Uzbek *sum*.

A well-worn path leads through the trees, thirty yards from the traffic lanes on either side. At first I ran through the January snow here, then the March mud and then the long grasses of April. May brought mowing crews, women with scythes chattering and slicing. Couples, elderly men, groups of women with grandchildren normally occupy the benches that are empty today. At the intersection with the next boulevard, large posters in Uzbek proclaim love of elders and the earth and the good traditional life.

My route reaches the monument to the 1966 earthquake and turns south around the Supreme Court building, along the central canal past outdoor restaurants that normally would be teeming with life but now stand empty. Ahead lies the national stadium, named Pakhtakor for the "cotton pickers," the keystone of the Uzbek economy in Soviet times as now. A few yards away across the canal stands the gleaming new white Senate building, normally with police guards. Today there is nobody at all.

The practice track at the stadium would normally have crowds of teen-aged Uzbek and Russian kids playing soccer, tossing the hammer or discus, or sprinting. Today the track too is deserted and I take my laps alone. The smell of ozone stings the nostrils.

There is too much to think about. The government has rather clumsily cut the internet links to the BBC and *New York Times* and censored Russian telecasts about Andijan, but it has been relatively easy for me to access international reports because the Uzbek government doesn't seem to know about the *San Jose Mercury* or the *Akron Beacon Journal* or hundreds of other international sites that carry the news.

We are here because my wife has come on a Fulbright fellowship. We can afford an apartment, so we have rented one. Cars operate as private taxis because their owners need the money. Teachers are paid little more than one U.S. dollar a day. There are twenty-five million people in this country, many of them very well-educated under the Soviet system. We have met scores, young and old, who speak Uzbek, Russian, English, and in some cases also Tajik, which is Persian. They know what is going on in the world and what is and is not happening in their country. The President of Uzbekistan has inherited a police- and KGB-driven system from the Soviets and uses it. He gives every sign of being about to confer a lifetime term of office on himself. Any dissent, even a neighborhood meeting outside the officially allowed structure, is considered militancy, Islamic militancy, and its leaders arrested. Almost every ethnic Uzbek or Tajik is a Muslim to some degree.

I could be cowering indoors, but I am not. Perhaps I don't realize the danger, but the atmosphere of control in Tashkent is so thorough that there really is little danger. I can't do anything about that, nor about the miserably depressed economy, but I can run. To run is to be able to run. Even under the black wool clouds the charged air is free to draw upon, carries the same oxygen as always for the fire in the legs that burns and travels forward. One does what one is able to do, even if all one can do is run. Running is learning, and not everything learned is pleasant, even on a run.

At home a warm shower, fragrant disks of marvelous round Uzbek bread, apricots, borscht. Our friends back home know more than we do about the Andijan business. But soon enough, we learn. The same afternoon that I ran under the thunderclouds, the police in Andijan opened fire on *thousands* of their own citizens, killing perhaps seven hundred. Only a hundred and forty dead, all of them young men who might pass for a threat perhaps, have been displayed by the government. One of our acquaintances has a best friend who was an eyewitness and the facts are told. There were hundreds of women and children among the victims and they were buried immediately, no one knows where. Soldiers did in fact finish off the wounded. The demonstrations were for justice, a better economy, a voice. A few apparently did say "in the name of God" but this was no Islamic militant gathering, or else the chant "God is great" would have been heard continuously and even the clumsily edited tapes released by the government show that it was not.[12]

There is no way to process human agony. Life is difficult enough without lies, deceit, brutality, the naked exercise of power. What does the mind of a human know, as it shuts down forever, of the relative worth that the world has accorded its particular life?

In the days to come, entire streets along my regular route are closed and filled in with parkland and trees. They happen to lie on the route to the Presidential Office. Tram tracks are taken up and replaced with heavy rails that can support military transport. Public employees in high positions all endorse the government account that only 141 died and all were Islamic militants.

What will be the future of the thousands of bright, motivated, articulate young people of Uzbekistan who are still looking for a better life for themselves and their country even as their government closes off the avenues to get there, filling those avenues with so-called security measures? Many of the students I met could excel at U.S. colleges if the route and money were only available.

We left Tashkent a few weeks later, slightly earlier than planned. The run of May 14 is still in my mind. It always will

---

[12] See the Human Rights Watch website for details.

be. What does it mean to run through something like that? What does it mean to run on an Antarctic glacier, or through the heat of South African reconciliation or Greek history, or acculturation in Japan, or Australian handicap racing, or Brazilian exuberance? One run, someday, will be my last. Will I know it at the time, will it matter? What will happen after that?

Sometimes, perhaps all the time, the only way to process the unanswerable questions in life is, simply, to take a deep breath and run.